In His Grip

A TRUE STORY OF A TEAM THAT WILL TAKE YOU DOWN AND LIFT YOU UP

Greg Hicks

Scripture quotations taken from the New American Standard Bible®, Copyright © 1960, 1962, 1963, 1968, 1971, 1972, 1973, 1975, 1977, 1995 by The Lockman Foundation. Used by permission. (www.Lockman.org)

Athletes in Action photos: Permission granted and provided by Athletes in Action, 651 Taylor Dr., Xenia, OH 45385

Oswald Chambers' quotes: Taken from *My Utmost for His Highest* by Oswald Chambers, Copyright 1935 by Dodd Mead & Col, renewed Copyright 1963 by the Oswald Chambers Publications Assn., Ltd., and is used by permission of Discovery House Publishers, Box 356, Grand Rapids, MI 49501. All rights reserved.

Arrowhead Springs photo: Permission granted and provided by CRU, Campus Crusade for Christ, Inc., 100 Lake Hart Dr., Orlando, FL 32832

ISBN: 978-1-4834-0971-9 (sc)
ISBN: 978-1-4834-0970-2 (e)

Library of Congress Control Number: 2014905349

Lulu Publishing Services rev. date: 08/18/2014

To the great Athletes in Action (AIA) wrestlers, their wives, and the support staff, who are truly mighty men and women of God and who have had a powerful impact on the lives of tens of thousands of people around the world.

Contents

Prologue

As we rode up the side of the mountain, forty miles outside the city of Beijing, the gondola moved slowly and quietly. Everyone in the group was deep in his or her own thoughts as each took advantage of the silence to relax and reflect. The group consisted of seventy-five people from twenty-eight countries who had gathered to attend the 2008 Olympic Games—the first Olympics ever in China.

When the gondola door opened, we walked toward the Great Wall of China—one of the Seven Wonders of the World. Once we reached the apex of the wall, people paused to snap pictures on their cell phones and digital cameras. I quickly gathered my four old friends for a photo to document another great time together.

It was amazing that this small group of best friends could get together at this appointed time. Precisely forty years earlier when we were twenty-two and twenty-three years old, John Klein, Larry Amundson, Gene and Frances Davis, and I, Greg Hicks, were recruits to a new unique athletic team. We became teammates on a brand-new all-star wrestling team of graduating college athletes sponsored by Athletes in Action (AIA), a Christian-based sports organization, and a division of Campus Crusade for Christ (CRU).

Incredible things had happened in the forty-year span to these wrestlers and their wives, along with numerous additional teammates along the way who made up the AIA wrestling team. God used the sport of wrestling to awaken millions of people around the world. The impact of knowing Christ personally, for each wrestler and wife, was real, and their story was presented to hundreds of thousands of people in person, using the attractive venue of sports and athletics. This is their story, God's story. These pages contain only a small portion of what God did through their ministry and outreach. Amazingly, the impact is still being felt to this day. The apostle Paul said, "We wrestle not against flesh and blood" (Ephesians 6:12), but the AIA team did just that as a platform to share their personal faith in Jesus Christ.

Why would God use a team of wrestlers to share His story of forgiveness and redemption? Maybe it is because amateur wrestlers are a special breed of athletes—possessing amazing tenacity and the mental discipline to "buffet their body," to suffer through intense workouts with no hope of real fame and fortune, as in other sports. And history illustrates that wrestlers always have been this way, according to a legend.

Forty Singing Wrestlers

In the days when the ruling passion of the Roman emperor Nero was the extermination of Christians, there served a band of soldiers known as the "Emperor's Wrestlers." Fine, stalwart men they were, picked from the best and bravest of the land, having been recruited from the great athletes of the Roman amphitheater.

In the amphitheater, they upheld the arms of the emperor against all challengers. Before each contest, they stood before the emperor's throne. Then through the courts of Rome rang their cry, "We, the wrestlers wrestling for thee, O emperor, to win for thee the victory and from thee, the victor's crown."

When the great Roman army was sent to fight in faraway Gaul, no soldiers were braver and more loyal than this band of wrestlers led by their centurion, Vespasian. But the news reached Nero, informing him that many of the wrestlers had accepted the Christian faith. To be a Christian meant death, even to those who served Nero best. Therefore, Nero's decree was straightway dispatched to the centurion

Vespasian, "If there be any among the soldiers who cling to the faith of the Christian, they must die."

The decree was received in the dead of winter. The wrestling soldiers were camped on the shore of a frozen inland lake. The winter had been hard, but the many hardships they had endured together served to unite them more closely. It was with a sinking heart that Vespasian read the emperor's message. Yet to a soldier there is one word supreme—that is duty.

Vespasian called the soldiers together and asked, "Are there any among you who cling to the faith of the Christian? If so, let him step forward." Forty wrestlers instantly stepped forward two paces, respectfully saluted, and stood at attention. Vespasian paused. He had not expected so many. "The decree has come from your emperor," he emphasized, "that any who cling to the faith of the Christian must die! For the sake of your country, your comrades, your loved ones, renounce this false faith." Not one of them moved. "Until sundown I shall await your answer," Vespasian replied. Sundown came. Again, the question was asked, "Are there among you who cling to the faith of the Christian? If so, let him step forward." Forty wrestlers stepped forward.

The forty wrestlers were stripped, and then, without a word, they wheeled, fell into columns of four, and marched toward the lake of ice. As they marched, they broke into the familiar chorus of the old arena chant, but this time they said, "Forty wrestlers, wrestling for Thee, O Christ, to win for Thee the victory and from Thee the victor's crown." Through the long hours of the night Vespasian stood by his campfire and waited. All through the long night there came to him fainter and fainter refrains from the wrestlers' song.

As morning drew near, one figure, overcome by exposure, crept quietly toward the fire. In the extremity of his suffering he renounced his Lord. Faintly but clearly from the darkness came the song, "Thirty-nine wrestlers, wrestling for Thee, O Christ, for Thee the victory and from Thee the victor's crown."

Vespasian looked into the darkness from whence came the familiar song of faith. This time perhaps he saw a great light shining in the darkness. Off came his helmet, down went his shield, and he sprang into the lake of ice, crying, "Forty wrestlers, wrestling for Thee, O Christ, to win for Thee the victory and from Thee, the victor's crown."

And the number of God's forty singing wrestlers was complete.

In His Grip,
Greg Hicks

**Great Wall of China—2008. Teammates
Gene Davis (and wife, Frances), John Klein,
Larry Amundson, and Greg Hicks.**

Introduction

Athletes in Action (AIA) is the sports ministry of Campus Crusade for Christ (CRU). Founder Dave Hannah and assistant director Pat Matrisciana developed a collegiate all-star wrestling team and basketball team in 1967. The wrestling team was a short-term summer team, but the basketball team successfully toured and competed during the full 1967–68 season against college teams across America. Dave and Pat envisioned traveling teams in many sports that would tour not only the United States but worldwide, using athletics as a platform to share their faith in Christ.

Since 1951, when Dr. Bill Bright founded the CRU organization at UCLA, college athletes were responsive to the message of Jesus Christ. Bill and his wife, Vonette, found the college campus was the fertile field they had hoped for as students began to respond. Very quickly several key student athletes joined the campus movement, including football players and star track athletes.

Dave and Pat had gotten a firsthand taste of big-time college wrestling having been former CRU college campus staff members at the University of Oklahoma (OU). The pulsating campus arena was electric as OU hosted the likes of wrestling powerhouses Oklahoma State and Iowa State of the Big Eight Conference before screaming crowds of five thousand fans.

Dave Hannah, being a former football player at Oklahoma State University, had seen crowds of eight thousand cheer his beloved Cowboys to several national wrestling championships. Dave became a Christian as a student and committed his life to Christ and to athletics. It was there he realized the power of sports personalities serving as role models. He further realized the influence athletes could have for the cause of Christ.

But there is a vast difference between one single athlete being a role model versus putting together a full-time team of Christian athletes to travel all over the world to compete. Eric Liddell in 1922, as an Olympic gold medalist for Great Britain in track and field, was a wonderful example of an individual athlete using his popularity to influence others for Christ. Earlier in 1891, Dr. James Naismith, an athletic instructor at the Springfield YMCA in Massachusetts, invented the game of basketball in order to "win men to the Master through the gym." Aside from a few summer mission tour teams, a full-fledged competing team of all Christian athletes had never been tried on a full-time basis prior to Dave Hannah's dream.

Despite the odds of success, Dave and Pat followed their instincts and sports vision to try their first international AIA team outreach. They chose wrestling as the sport and Japan as their destination. They recruited UCLA wrestling coach Dave Hollinger to take a college all-star team of Christian wrestlers for a summer tour in Japan. John Klein, a big-time wrestler from the University of Minnesota was part of the team.

In midsummer 1967, the US college all-star wrestlers competed against the best that Japan had to offer. The team shared their faith in Christ with fellow athletes, officials, and fans wherever possible, and came back to the United States convinced their original concept of using sports teams to share the message of Christ to impact people lives would work. The next logical step was to duplicate the strategy in the United States using full-time teams.

In 1967 college students were restless and yearning for change. Big change! The hippie culture was spreading, and young people were joining college campus radicals in rebelling against the US government, their parents, and anything that was labeled "the Establishment." The clarion cries of the hippies were "free love" and "peace," while the radicals pushed young men to burn their draft cards in protest of the Vietnam War. Young women were burning their bras in support of equal rights for women. Marijuana and LSD were replacing alcohol as the stimulants of choice. The leftist Yippy leader Jerry Ruben said, "We were constantly stoned and tripping on every drug known to man."

"Revolution" was the cry across the landscape. It was becoming clear that the massive initial wave of baby boomers turning twenty-one were not going to be like their parents. Nothing would ever be the same again in America. California was the fertile ground for all the campus social movements. The movements were spreading quickly from the west coast to the east. "Freedom" had been the cry in Boston two hundred years earlier from the tyranny of the British king's edicts and taxes. By 1968 it was a cry of freedom from moral codes, freedom from having to go to war, and freedom from the laws of culture, civil government, and parents.

Racial unrest spread nationwide, and the peaceful demonstrations led by Martin Luther King Jr, who was assassinated on April 4, 1968, opened doors for more militant leaders such as Huey Newton and Eldridge Cleaver to take over the once-peaceful Civil Rights movement.

President Lyndon Johnson was experiencing great difficulty balancing his Great Society agenda—committing billions of tax dollars to help "stamp out poverty" while expanding the Vietnam War. Then on March 31, 1968, he announced he would not seek the nomination for reelection for president of the United States.

Furthermore, while in Los Angeles campaigning as a Democrat Party candidate for president, Robert Kennedy, the brother of President John F. Kennedy, was assassinated on June 6 by Sirhan Sirhan.

Later that summer, knowing the radicals were planning huge anti-war protests, Chicago officials brought in an additional twenty thousand police and National Guardsmen to fend off the trouble as violence erupted at the Democratic National Convention. In Miami on August 8, after the Republican National Convention nominated

Richard Nixon as their presidential candidate, race riots broke out in the city.

America was in great turmoil. The fabric of the American culture was being pulled apart by large and dynamic forces. The civilization seemed to be unraveling. What could be done? How could a revolution start that could change society for the better? These burning questions were making a new generation hungry for answers.

One small spark of change would come that summer from a most unlikely source, in an unlikely location. It seemed California was also going to be a place for another revolution. Fifty miles east of Los Angeles in the foothills near San Bernardino, a gathering took place with a small group of amateur wrestlers and a few wives. A few men obsessed with a vision had spent a year of work and effort to see their vision come true from nothing but a faith in the living God. These fearless AIA leaders were going to provide some long-awaited answers for this restless generation, and it would emanate from, of all things, a group of athletes.

Chapter 1

The Beginning of a Dream

*In the history of God's work, you will nearly always find
that it started from the obscure, the unknown, the ignored.*
—Oswald Chambers

March 21–23, 1968

The annual NCAA Division I Collegiate Wrestling Championship
was a flurry of activity on a cold weekend in State College,
Pennsylvania, home of the Penn State Nittany Lions. Almost 350
wrestlers from dozens of college teams across America were going
through the tournament brackets in head-to-head matchups on eight
mats that dotted the arena floor like a checkerboard.

Among the fifteen thousand fans were two men, Pat Matrisciana
and John Klein, who came with a special mission in mind—to recruit
top seniors for a brand-new Athlete in Action (AIA) wrestling team.
What better place to recruit than the NCAA wrestling tournament?
The men had worked diligently, contacting as many recruits as they
could before the event.

It was hoped that several young wrestlers would become the
first recruits of their long, hard efforts. Pat was acting like a man
possessed as he gazed over the arena floor, which was loaded with
top-flight wrestlers. He was determined to climb up any hill or run
through any wall to launch this new venture before the fall of 1968,

the beginning of the next college wrestling season. He came to Penn State fully prepared and fully "prayed up," expecting God to come through for him—if it was meant to be.

Pat's sidekick recruiter was John Klein. John was a 1967 graduate of the University of Minnesota. He had joined the staff of AIA during the previous summer for the inaugural All-Star Wrestling Team tour to Japan. At this moment at Penn State, John *was* the AIA wrestling team—one wrestler who came with Pat with dreams of recruiting some teammates.

Three athletes on Pat and John's recruiting list were Gene Davis, a 1966 NCAA champ from wrestling powerhouse Oklahoma State; Larry Amundson, a Division II NCAA champ from Mankato State (now named Minnesota State); and Greg Hicks, a two-time ACC champ from North Carolina State University. Little did John or Pat know that these young wrestlers, fresh out of college, would someday be used to forge the leadership of a legacy that still lives and thrives.

Until that weekend at Penn State, the idea of a full-time all-star wrestling team touring the United States, competing with top college teams and using sports as a platform for sharing stories of life-changing faith in Jesus Christ was a pipe dream. Who would ever believe this far-fetched plan would come to fruition? No one! But God would soon arrange a series of events in His divine providence to create the spark needed to make it become a reality … and quickly, too!

Pat Matrisciana was not a wrestler but was a huge wrestling fan. His assignment as assistant director of AIA was to recruit the first team. It started with John Klein, a farm kid from Tracy, Minnesota. John was from a large family, and every kid was expected to do chores—yes, even in the subzero temperatures of the dead of winter. Lots of Lutheran families dotted the landscape of rural Minnesota, but John was a Catholic kid with a German heritage. Sheltered from big-city life, John grew up a tough, strong kid with natural strength developed from hard labor on the farm. That strength made him good at wrestling, a tough man's sport.

On graduating from high school, John knew he wanted three things: to get a college degree; to wrestle in college; and to leave the farm life to his parents and siblings. John chose to attend the University of Minnesota in Minneapolis, a city with a population one hundred times larger than Tracy, a town in which he would never return to live.

Unfamiliar with big-city life, John had to learn some things the hard way. Once he took a new date out to a nice restaurant for dinner. After ordering his steak, baked potato, and salad, the waitress asked him what kind of dressing he would like. John was unaware there was more than one, so he asked what kinds they had. The waitress listed French, Italian, blue cheese, and a number of others. John was bewildered by those choices. He was thinking of asking the waitress if they had the "regular turkey dressing." Back home on the farm, the only time John's family had dressing was with turkey at the Thanksgiving meal. Unsure of the dressing choices, John asked his date what she was having, and she replied, "French." So John said he would like French as well, though he wondered what French dressing would taste like with his steak. After the meal was served, John discovered there was no dressing with his steak. He tried to get the waitress's attention to ask if he could have the dressing served with his steak, but fortunately the waitress was busy. John decided he probably would not like the French version of dressing anyway, so he enjoyed the steak dinner without incident. John faced a little cultural training as he made his way through the university.

John was a tactical thinker both in the classroom and on the wrestling mat, where he excelled. He also had another encounter at "The U" that was totally unexpected. A contact at college shared a concept with John as he joined a small group to study the Bible. Growing up Catholic, the concept of a personal relationship with Jesus was foreign to him. He knew Jesus as a historical figure the priest talked about when John occasionally attended Mass or confessions. No one had told him God's Son, Jesus, could be known in a personal way. Soon John was convinced this was possible and asked Jesus into his life. John's life quickly began to change direction. A Christian group on campus, Campus Crusade for Christ (CRU), began to mentor him in the Bible and teach him the principles of a Christian life. Eventually, John decided to forgo his career plans and join the CRU staff. He applied and was accepted, but not before a face-to-face meeting with CRU founder and director, Dr. Bill Bright.

Dr. Bright asked John to resign from AIA because a number of CRU's Latin American leaders did not want someone with a Catholic background on the staff. John told Dr. Bright he could fire him, but he would not voluntarily resign. John shared with Dr. Bright how he became a believer and that he believed God wanted him to be part of AIA to share with others how he discovered a personal relationship with God. After some discussion, Dr. Bright agreed to let John continue on as a new staff member.

John Klein became the first and only member of the wrestling team in the summer of 1967. AIA national director Dave Hannah and Pat Matrisciana now had to recruit a full-time team of nine other athletes and a coach. Then, on top of that, they had to create a college schedule. They circled March 21–23, 1968, on their calendar for a trip to Penn State to get commitments from recruits. They needed wrestlers, and fast. That weekend was to be a catalyst to building the AIA wrestling team.

A second Minnesota kid was also heading to Penn State. Larry Amundson had grown up in the small town of Windom, the son of good, Lutheran parents of Swedish stock. He was a short, stocky blond kid with a low center of gravity—perfect for wrestling. He attended church with his family, and at a youth retreat as a youngster he prayed for Christ to come into his life. He wanted to go to college to be a teacher and coach someday, so he chose a good nearby Division II college, Mankato State (Minnesota State). Larry was also a social animal! He loved people, parties, and fun.

At Mankato State, he relentlessly pursued his goal of becoming a teacher and coach, along with wrestling and being a frat boy. The fraternity life fit Larry like a glove, with a social life too good to ignore, parties every weekend, and lots of girls. As a well-known and popular college athlete, he tried hard to successfully balance academics, athletics, and fraternity life.

Spiritual things got crowded out a bit in college. Deep inside he knew God was there, but a guilt complex became his constant companion. Two weeks before the NCAA wrestling tournament, Larry won the Small College (Division II) National Wrestling Championship. He became a big man on campus. Larry made it to the finals at Penn State against the Division I big boys, only to lose a heartbreaker in the last seconds of the championship match.

The AIA recruiters, Pat and John, had been told before the tournament that Larry was a Christian. An all-American wrestler and a Christian kid sounded like a prospect to Pat and John. They saw Larry as a building block for an all-star team, which would tour the United States and the world, sharing the team's faith in Christ. They laid their heavy recruiting pitch on Larry. Larry listened intently but somewhat skeptically. He asked Pat and John, "Who pays for all this?" They looked Larry in the eye and answered, "Every wrestler raises his own salary and support from donors." Larry was student teaching that semester, and with his newfound fame as a wrestling champ, he knew high schools would line up to hire him as a teacher and wrestling coach. A skeptical Larry wondered, *Why would anyone in his right mind join the AIA wrestling team?*

Another potential top recruit was Gene Davis, a Montana mountain boy from Missoula, who had just married his longtime girlfriend, Frances, who was finishing her home economics degree at the University of Montana. Gene grew up as the younger of two sons in a family that loved hunting, fishing, and wrestling. He started wrestling at a young age, and by the time he finished high school, he was a four-time state high school champion in several weight classes. Small and spunky, no one could touch him on the wrestling mat. He attracted recruiters from big-time wrestling colleges, including perennial powerhouse Oklahoma State. Coach Myron Roderick loved the spunk of young Gene and signed him with a full scholarship!

Gene's freshman year was spent being homesick. He longed for the lush beauty of the Rocky Mountains as he looked across the treeless prairie of Oklahoma from his dorm room. He missed his girlfriend. He was also getting beat up every day by the NCAA champions on the OSU team during wrestling practice.

Unfortunately for Gene, two teammates nearest his weight class were national champions, and one was an Olympic champion from Japan. Gene became "cannon fodder" for these two guys early on and was pounded on every single day. But he kept coming back for more, and by his junior year he was crowned the NCAA Champion in 1966 at the National Tournament at Iowa State University. The Rocky Mountain boy had made it to the top of the athletic mountain!

He attended church camp at a young age and accepted Christ into his life. His family was one that did not emphasize spiritual things, but Gene, along with Frances, tried to live the Christian life the best he could. He got involved with CRU on the OSU campus.

In 1968, while Frances was finishing up her degree, Gene was in graduate school and coaching at the University of Montana for a semester. Since the Vietnam War was raging, he and Frances thought long and hard about him joining the army and going to officer candidate school. In March, Gene decided to go to the NCAA Tournament at Penn State with his high school coach one last time before he joined the military.

Meanwhile, Pat and John had great hopes of recruiting Gene, who not only was a national champ but was coached by one of the greatest coaches of all time, Myron Roderick. This would be a "home run" for the new AIA wrestling team. Pat and John tracked down Gene and challenged him seriously about his future. Gene listened with interest but was somewhat uncomfortable with the whole concept. He was planning to enlist in the army and thought this AIA wrestling team would likely never happen anyway.

Lastly there was Greg Hicks. Greg's experience at the NCAA Wrestling Tournament was a little different from the other potential recruits'. He was a good wrestler from the basketball powerhouse NC State University, where he was majoring in chemical engineering. He was a two-time ACC champ but had never placed in the Nationals. Penn State was his last chance to change his destiny, as he was upset in the ACC finals just two weeks before. Unfortunately, Greg's confidence was shaken and it did not go well at Penn State. He lost in the first round.

Greg married his childhood sweetheart, Sue, in June 1967 just after his junior year. Their goal of a happy marriage lasted only a few weeks, when things started going poorly. Greg was used to being successful and did not handle the failing marriage well. Simultaneously, at a summer job in a chemical lab, a coworker started talking to Greg about knowing Jesus Christ. Being a typical southern boy, Greg attended church his entire life but had long given up on his church's harsh demands. But now he was desperate and his coworker was telling him that Christ could personally solve his problem if only Greg would "surrender his life to the Lord." One night in desperation, Greg prayed and gave it all—his life, his troubled marriage, and his future to Christ. Suddenly everything changed! Seeing the difference in Greg's behavior, Sue gave her life to Christ two weeks later.

In the fall of Greg's senior year, his wrestling coach gave him a magazine after practice one day. It was the first *Athletes in Action* magazine, a new publication with articles about their wrestling team touring Japan and sharing their faith in Christ. Greg was fascinated. He wrote an enquiry letter to AIA. Pat Matrisciana responded and said, "See you at Penn State, and we'll talk." Even with Pat knowing that Greg had suffered the bitter defeats at the ACC finals and at the NCAA Tournament, he still wanted him to join the new team.

After the Nationals, each recruit headed back to his home. As fate would have it, Gene and Larry caught a ride to the airport in the same car. The ever-social Larry asked Gene to lunch while they waited for their flights. As they chatted about wrestling and the tournament, one of them brought up the AIA wrestling team. They were full of questions, such as, "What about a coach? What about the schedule? What about raising our own support?"

As they finished, Larry asked, "Do you think this could ever possibly work?"

Gene replied, "No, I don't think so."

"Me neither," Larry said.

And with that they boarded their planes for home.

In truth, no one knew if this new team would fly or fail. But Pat and John had been outstanding ambassadors, spreading the word about the future AIA wrestling team to many wrestlers and coaches. They actually believed God could raise up a team. Could it ever happen, really?

> "For the dream comes through much effort."
> (Ecclesiastes 5:3)

Chapter 2

The Team Appears

The danger is to glorify men; Jesus says we are to lift Him up.
—Oswald Chambers

June 9–15, 1968
Arrowhead Springs, Southern California

John Klein and Pat Matrisciana forged ahead with the vision of starting a full-time AIA wrestling team with plans to wrestle a major college schedule in the autumn of 1968. However, several key ingredients were still missing—like a head coach, the wrestlers, the finances, and the schedule! Those large obstacles never seemed to faze Pat or John nor slow them from pressing forward to reach their goals. They began challenging several top college wrestling coaches with the idea of bringing this mythical all-star team to their campuses for a dual meet competition.

Surprisingly, college wrestling coaches all over America loved the idea of scheduling a team of topnotch Christian athletes. The coaches realized it was a rare opportunity to have their program matched up against some great wrestlers that did not count in their official win-loss records. They figured they could draw many new fans from the campus and the community with the enhanced publicity of the visiting star-studded AIA team coming to town. They could also have the AIA boys practice with their team for a couple of days, which would make their wrestlers only better against that kind of competition. Plus, AIA wrestlers would have a very positive influence on their own wrestlers, character-wise.

Another pleasant surprise was the number of coaches who personally embraced Christianity. A number of top college coaches stepped up to schedule this "team" and were prepared to print the match in their media guides to promote it. They also stepped up to pay the customary travel honorarium for a visiting team. AIA was desperately short of cash to fund their operation, and any money for expenses would be critical for success. Incredibly, the first year's schedule included Oklahoma, Oklahoma State, Cal Poly, and Iowa State—all top ten teams—among several other colleges. Now if AIA only had a team and a coach!

Soon after the Nationals, another ex-wrestler from Colorado State College (now University of Northern Colorado) was planning to join CRU staff. He was a high school wrestling coach from Arvada, Colorado, a suburb of Denver. Doug Rickard had been out of college for three years, teaching and coaching in high school. He also had a wife named Jackie and one child. He was comfortable becoming a CRU regular staff member—until he met Pat and John. In their meeting, Pat and John challenged Doug to return to competition. The idea of going back on the mat to grapple on a touring Christian team was very persuasive. But the idea of putting on a wrestling uniform to compete again? Doug thought, *No way.*

Pat and John issued a challenge for Doug as they explained, "This is your one and final chance to use your wrestling talent for the glory of God! Imagine, you travel around the United States in a car for four months at a time, stay in other people's houses, raise your own support for a family of three—no problem!"

Despite some serious anxiety and much prayer, Doug and Jackie accepted the challenge! Now the AIA team—or should that be the AIA tag team?—had two confirmed wrestlers. Unfortunately, there were eight more weight classes in college wrestling to fill.

The initial team launch and final recruiting promotional event was an inaugural AIA wrestling camp scheduled for the week of June 9–15, 1968, at Arrowhead Springs in San Bernardino, California, at CRU headquarters. Any wrestler who had ever remotely expressed any interest in the AIA wrestling team was invited to attend. If they had ever considered following Christ and were even a marginally good wrestler, they received an invitation to the camp. Pat's theory was that he could convince a wrestler to follow Christ once he got to Arrowhead Springs, or at least in the car on the way up the mountain from the airport. (That indeed actually happened to a couple of recruits!) Pat cajoled, begged, and challenged wrestlers to show up, and he was not above dropping names to impress these young athletes. Wrestlers all over America were getting phone calls and letters encouraging them to attend the camp.

Arrowhead Springs truly was a special place and a good drawing card for the recruits. The former luxury hotel was the former "hot spot" of Hollywood stars in the 1940s and '50s. Dr. Bill Bright and CRU had purchased it for a bargain-basement price a few years earlier, by faith that God would supply the money. And God did!

Pat and John were surprised at the number of young men who promised they would show up to Arrowhead Springs, even if only for a couple of days. Would the five days of wrestling camp be the foundation to forge the new team? Clearly with the wrestling season less than a scant six months away, this was a make-it-or-break-it event for the new team.

The biggest surprise was how God had worked out circumstances in the lives of certain individuals to attract them to Southern California.

Many wrestlers such as Bob Anderson, a new Christian from the surfer culture of Southern California, along with his wife, Janet, were invited to attend. He was a high school state champion who had wrestled at NAIA wrestling powerhouse Adams State and became an NAIA All-American. Mitsuo Nakai, a graduate student at the University of Washington, was coming. He was a collegiate wrestling champion in Japan. There was Doug Smith, a former Oregon High School champ, who wrestled at the University of Washington and Loren Miller, a mountain man from Northern California who wrestled at San Jose State. Several other wrestlers and coaches came out of curiosity to simply check it out.

None of the three recruits who met with Pat and John at Penn State at the NCAA Wrestling Tournament were planning to join the new AIA team. But God had a different plan for each of them. Early recruit Greg Hicks had accepted a glamorous job working as a chemical engineer on Polaris submarines at the Newport News, Virginia, shipyard. His wife, Sue, was happy with that decision. Greg's mom and dad were happy, especially since his dad had worked in the Newport News shipyard during World War II.

Everyone was happy—except Greg! He repeatedly asked God, even as a new Christian, to give him direction and peace with his career choice. He chose the Polaris job, but inner peace never came. Even as the moving van company representative sat in their living room setting up the date to move them from Raleigh to Virginia, Greg knew deep down that it would never happen. Against the hopes of family and friends, Greg and Sue finally decided, even with some initial anxiety, to turn down the high-paying starting salary and travel by faith to Southern California to investigate the AIA team to see if it was a legitimate organization. With the decision, peace finally came, at least for Greg!

Larry Amundson, who was still checking out coaching jobs, had talked about the AIA wrestling team with his mom and dad. His parents started talking to their friends about Larry's offer from AIA. A local businessman quizzed Larry about the new team. Larry mentioned that each AIA team member had to find people to donate financially to support their efforts. A couple of days after the conversation a check showed up from the businessman, paying for Larry's initial trip to Arrowhead Springs.

Oh my, Larry thought, *now I might have to go to California!* Larry continually thought back to his first meeting with Pat and

John at Penn State. He wondered, *Who told them I'm a Christian? I certainly haven't lived the Christian life very successfully in college.* Yet he found himself packing for the long drive from Minnesota to Southern California in his newly purchased Chevy Camaro—all the time wondering if he was making a big mistake. Even after arriving at camp, Larry kept his new car "pointed east" in the parking lot at all times, just in case an early exit was needed to hustle back home.

Gene Davis did not attend the AIA camp because he was still planning to join the army.

The AIA camp schedule was a combination of morning classes and afternoon workouts. In the mornings they heard great Christian teachers speak about how to live the Christian life. Afternoons consisted of wrestling workouts. They worked out on borrowed wrestling mats from a local high school laid out on a small outdoor basketball court near the "village" of dorm rooms at Arrowhead Springs.

The wrestling sessions were, in a word, weird. There was no coach to lead a structured practice so everyone just made up practice as they went. The oppressive smog that nestled in the foothills made the wrestlers almost choke after a few minutes of a workout. The only good thing about the smog was that it kept the hot sun from heating up the mats too much during the hot desert afternoons, where the average temperatures hovered around 102 degrees. To say the least, it was quite an unimpressive start as far as athletic facilities for the big-time Christian all-star team.

The morning's spiritual training was what most impressed the recruits. Many of these young believers had never heard such practical biblical teaching before. The great teachers grabbed everyone's attention. One evening a popular speaker and famous author, Hal Lindsey, spoke about the biblical accuracy of prophesy in world history and current events. He blew away the wrestlers and their wives with his message. Many of the young recruits realized they were in for much more than they had anticipated. Wrestling was very important, but the spiritual side of Athletes in Action was going to be more amazing!

At the end of the fifth day of camp, each person had to immediately decide whether to stay or go home, to join the team or not. Each man and woman had to deal with some serious anxiety and even fear in making this big decision, which would dramatically affect their immediate and near-term future. Careers choices were on the line, money and income were on the line, and moving to Southern California was mandatory to join the team. Pat and John answered dozens of questions from the new recruits and kept encouraging them to commit.

For some recruits it was all so new and different. Greg and Sue Hicks struggled and debated over the goal of sharing their faith with others, plus moving three thousand miles from North Carolina. The wrestling excited Greg, but they had never been around such mature Christians.

Larry Amundson kept wondering if he should go back to Minnesota and coach like he had planned.

Janet Anderson and Jackie Rickard were anxious about taking small children on the road for weeks at a time and staying in other people's homes on tour.

All of them knew there was risk in the decision. Joining this team was not going to lead them to a normal lifestyle of leisure and comfort, but the challenge and attractiveness of wrestling on a team representing Christ was very compelling.

John and Pat were very excited when several recruits committed to join, despite the fear and anxiety. Maybe God was going to do something with this new group of men and women after all! By July 4 the first AIA wrestling team photo was taken. Eight men and three wives had tentatively committed to two years of being on the first AIA wrestling team.

However, there was no coach in the first team photo.

In the late summer, Gene Davis was at a high school wrestling camp in Washington helping his former college coach. He figured he could earn a few bucks, coach a little, and have a nice semi-vacation at the camp. But God had other plans for this particular wrestling camp. One of the clinicians just happened to be Japanese collegiate champion Mitsuo Nakai. He had just returned from seven weeks at Arrowhead Springs and was really excited about his time with his new AIA teammates. He encouraged Gene to join the team, saying, "It was great! It was awesome!"

He and Gene talked about it several times. Gene headed back to Missoula praying and thinking hard about the army and what Mitsuo had said. The army application was filled out, ready to deliver to the recruiting officer. After much prayer and great debate, the army application was never delivered because Gene and his wife, Frances, agreed that AIA was in their future, at least for now. Gene contacted Pat about his decision, and suddenly the team had a potential coach.

Gene joined the team two months later while Frances stayed behind to finish her degree and student teach. Gene agreed to become the AIA head coach and also compete as a wrestler. Despite Gene and Larry being NCAA All-Americans, the team was not exactly the high-powered all-star team that Pat, John, and Dave Hannah had envisioned, but it was the team God wanted. God was going to take this motley crew of men and women just as they were and would begin a twenty-year journey of building wrestlers and their wives into committed followers of Christ and wrestling champions. The young recruits would become the catalyst for great and mighty things! No one could have imagined then what was to come.

The team was comprised of very ordinary people and even some "misfits." Each person was from lower- to middle-class families, without a social pedigree to brag about. But they had athletic talent, big hearts, and a desire to serve God in a most unique way. That was all God needed. Of all the pools of wrestlers in the world, and of all the athletes who had been contacted and recruited by Pat and John, God had attracted exactly enough to meet the NCAA standard of ten different weight classes to form a competing team.

The first AIA Team consisted of:

Larry Amundson, Mankato State   John Klein, Minnesota

Bob Anderson, Adams State   Loren Miller, San Jose State

Gene Davis, Oklahoma State   Mitsuo Nakai, Waseda University, Japan

John Hansen, Iowa State   Doug Rickard, Colorado State College

Greg Hicks, North Carolina State Doug Smith, Washington

A coach, a complete team, and a college wrestling schedule! Who would have thought it possible?

"There is an appointed time for everything.
And there is a time for every event under heaven"
(Ecclesiastes 3:1)

Chapter 3

Let the Training Begin

If we are to live as disciples, we have to
remember that noble things are difficult.
—Oswald Chambers

Summer 1968
San Bernardino, California

During the months of June and July 1968, the new AIA wrestling team was a flurry of activity. Once the wrestlers and several wives had made the decision to be on the first AIA team, they had to apply and officially be accepted to become CRU staff members. CRU had two key basic standards for a new staff member: a heart for God, and a teachable spirit.

Of course there were other new staff requirements as well. With any athlete "signing" to a team, sometimes concessions had to be made. In this group of wrestlers and wives, a couple of wrestlers had not yet graduated from college, which was a normal requirement. They all expressed faith in Christ, but some had not been believers of Jesus Christ as their personal Savior for at least a year—another requirement. They also had to satisfy a psychological personality profile that indicated they had behavioral traits favorable for following the chain of command, having effective social skills, and possessing persuasive skills with others. They may not have all been "qualified," but they were committed to learning these critical skills. They had wrestling talent and could be "coached up" on the spiritual things as well. All the recruits were accepted for new staff training that summer.

To advance the skills needed for being a CRU staff member, each person attended the Institute of Biblical Studies (IBS). The four weeks at IBS consisted of intense training similar to a seminary summer school curriculum, which was taught by seminary professors and graduates. The classes included the study of theology, books of the Bible, and Bible study techniques. IBS was followed by one week of new staff training and two weeks of senior staff training with classes on public speaking, learning how to raise financial support, improving communication skills, and becoming confident in how to lead others to Christ. CRU's goal was to offer two months of spiritual "boot camp"—a fast track—so these young recruits would be fully equipped to follow Jesus' command to go into all the world and make disciples, and be witnesses to the uttermost parts of the world (Matthew 28:19–20; Acts 1:8). The transition from wide-eyed athletes to full-blown missionaries for Christ would be complete, at least through phase one! Two more summers of training were to follow, assuming the wrestlers stayed with the team. Just like marines, the "boot camp" would make them fighting machines ready to do battle for God against any challengers on or off the mat!

Part of the requirements of the fast-track training was to share one's faith in Christ on the beautiful beaches of Southern California. The team took a bus to Huntington Beach for a day of talking about their faith to total strangers who were enjoying a day on the beach. To the muscular athletic wrestlers, the thought of this assignment was horrifying. To walk up to total strangers and talk to them about Jesus Christ was equally as tough as going to the center of the mat to wrestle in a packed arena. They were overcome by nothing short of fear and anxiety as they headed for the beach! There was no way out of this required exercise during staff training. God was about to give on-the-job training—a reality check apart from classroom academic training. There is no perfect formula to "witness" to others, but one simply needs to be willingly prepared, courageous, and bold. They nervously hopped off the bus and went out two by two to talk to folks on the beach.

Team members Bob Anderson and Mitsuo Nakai faced the day in their own unique way. Effervescent tough-guy and surfer-dude Bob Anderson was in his element. That day Bob and his witnessing partner, Mitsuo, decided they needed to draw a crowd. There was no fear for these two wrestlers.

Bob found an abandoned board lying on the sand and announced to the beachcombers, "Come and see a Japanese wrestler break a wooden board with his bare hands."

Of course Mitsuo had no martial arts training, but it really did not seem to matter! Soon a crowd drew near to see this amazing feat. Mitsuo charged the board Bob was holding and broke it in half. The crowd went wild with applause.

Bob turned away from the crowd and discovered his chest was blistered from the abrasion, and he picked splinters out of his sore and tender skin. But no matter, Bob and Mitsuo gathered their thoughts and started talking to bystanders about having a personal relationship with Christ.

After the day on the beach, team members rode back to Arrowhead Springs on the bus simply amazed at how open and willing people were to talk to them about spiritual things.

After IBS and staff training ended, everyone was cut loose to go home with a goal of returning in just eight weeks with their financial support. Single men had to raise $4,000 for a year while married couples had to raise $6,000 from donors who wanted to give financially to support their work in the nonprofit AIA organization. (Equivalent in today's dollars: $22,700 for married couples and $15,100 for singles.) At first glance it seemed like bad news—to the wrestlers! The first challenge was that no team member could count on his or her highly anticipated college graduate salaries. The other challenge was that each team member had to raise every dollar by asking other people to donate money. It was called "living by faith." No easy task!

Raising support was the mechanism the AIA wrestling team used to draw a line in the sand. The logic was if God had led them to the team, the support money would come as they began to "ask and receive." The team leaders trusted that God would provide financially, so each wrestler would report on October 1, 1968, to San Bernardino in decent athletic shape, as well as financially and spiritually sound … at least in theory.

The recruits were of different sizes and weights. This was not a coincidence but God's perfect plan. Heavyweight was an issue, but Bob Anderson and Larry Amundson could float weight classes from as low as 177 pounds to the heavyweight class, giving up 50 to 100 pounds to their opponent. No one promised it would be easy. After all, David had his Goliath!

Pat's recruiting continued after the summer as he landed a lightweight wrestler from Iowa State. His name was John Hansen, and he could wrestle in the 130-pound weight class. He was a place winner in the NCAA Tournament, but he was a new believer. Plus he had missed the summer staff training, meaning he did not have time or the skills to raise his financial support in time to report. No matter! The new rookie would be trained "on the fly" while touring with the AIA team throughout the United States. The AIA teammates would have to share their meager salaries to help meet John's financial needs.

Because of scant funds and a low budget, the AIA wrestling team would be driving to virtually every scheduled wrestling match. The team's driving schedule included the western half of the United States from California to Oklahoma to Washington to Colorado and back to Southern California. Later the team had to fly to Iowa State and then drive to Missouri and Illinois to close out the season. Convenience was not always on the travel agenda, as the young team would soon learn. A couple of all-nighters were included in the driving schedule. Sleep was optional on many occasions. A team bus? Forget it! The team members drove their own cars everywhere and spent their own money most of the time for gasoline and cheap motels.

What about practice gear, team uniforms, a practice squad, and a place to practice? When an athletic team is created out of thin air, the normal expectations are not normal anymore. Dave, Pat, and John cut a deal with the San Bernardino Junior College coach for a "borrowed" practice facility. Part of the agreement with the junior college coach was the AIA team had to occasionally practice with his wrestling team, but practice was at different times every day based on who was using the mat room. The AIA team could also use the college track for running, as long as the Southern California smog did not kill them on the spot!

Once the travel season started in mid-November, the team was going to be on the road almost constantly for four months. That presented other problems. How would the wrestlers and their wives rent an apartment for a full year only to live in it half the year? How would three married couples make a home feel like a home with such a bizarre traveling schedule? How would they get their mail? How would they pay their bills on time or deposit a check?

Money or lack thereof was always an issue for individuals and the team. Gene Davis and John Hansen, having missed the summer staff training, would arrive in October in San Bernardino woefully short of their full financial needs. Loren Miller arrived short of full support as well. No wrestler was flush with cash in his account. But the wrestling season was starting in early November, so they drove in on a "wing and a prayer," learning to raise finances as they went ... literally living by faith. The wrestlers were about to learn this was no college full-ride scholarship with the AIA wrestling team. It was to be more like survive and advance.

Raising support was a challenge and a blessing as it turned out for each wrestler and his wife. They were told at staff training to list all the friends and contacts they thought might be interested back home. Next they were taught the techniques of contacting prospective supporters and arranging an appointment to present the opportunity. Just like in wrestling or any other sport, it is one thing to be coached but quite another to implement and apply the training. Intimidation and fear gridlocked a few of the recruits at first, but with weekly phone calls from Pat and John from headquarters, the wrestlers initiated the task of raising financial support. They had about eight weeks to get the task done. After a few weeks of effort, each had stories of disappointment and success as people actually lined up to give financially to their new venture. Dozens of little miracles began to take place in each wrestler's two-month journey of raising support. God did show His power and sovereignty to bring new people into the wrestlers' lives to support their effort on the college campus.

One such story of God's care happened to Greg and Sue Hicks in North Carolina. They faithfully called all the people on their list and found they were not even close to reaching their financial goal. They had hit a brick wall after a couple of weeks with no additional donor prospects left to call. When in doubt, they were taught to pray and believe God would supply all their needs. Suddenly out of the blue, they got a call from Ricky Mill, who played on the AIA basketball team and had visited them just before Greg graduated that spring, to encourage them to join AIA.

Ricky was from Georgia but told them to call a Mrs. Smith in Raleigh. Her name had been passed along to him by someone, and he had been told she may be a good person to contact. Greg called Mrs. Smith and told her about the brand-new AIA wrestling team. She listened and said she might want to hear more and that having daughters in college she was concerned about the campuses in America.

Greg and Sue went to her house where she and her husband sat quietly in their family room listening to their story.

Suddenly Mrs. Smith said, "Oh, my, this is fabulous!" She looked over at her husband and said, "We have to help these people!" She told Greg and Sue to come back in one week and plan to spend several days and nights in their home. She would have some key people for them to meet.

The next week Mrs. Smith took them into the offices of some of the most influential people in town and to women's Bible studies. Even though she had only known Greg and Sue for one week, she proceeded to tell her contacts they "should support these two young people," and that they were "Christian pioneers out there talking to the students on the campuses of America." By the end of a week Greg and Sue had jumped to almost reaching 75 percent of their financial goal.

And it did not stop there. Over the next few years, every time they came home to continue raising financial support, Mrs. Smith had more people for them to meet. One of her friends gave Greg and Sue a car with only 25,000 miles on it to replace their old 1957 Pontiac with 150,000 miles and four bald tires, affectionately called "The Bomb." God did exactly as they had been told at staff training—that if you were supposed to be in AIA, God would make it happen. And He did, using a perfect stranger!

Pat and John raised some of the team's financial support and borrowed some money from CRU to buy team uniforms and some practice gear for the team. The college dual-meet honorariums did not add up to anywhere close to paying for the first year's touring budget. The team members by default would have to drive their own cars across America and stay mostly in strangers' homes while competing against some of the best universities in the land. Those small monthly salary checks did not go far either—$285 for single staff; $425 for married staff. This "living by faith" business was now being applied by each person. God would have to provide for this team to get through the very first year or it would collapse before year two could even begin.

As the team members reported to San Bernardino, everyone began searching for housing. Gene Davis, whose wife was finishing her degree in Montana, had a novel housing plan for himself and the single wrestlers. He and John Klein talked an owner of an old rundown mountain cabin into a tradeoff. The single guys and Gene would clean up the old cabin and renovate it to make it livable in exchange for a one-year low-cost lease. The cabin was a couple of miles up the mountain from the Arrowhead Springs headquarters, so it was convenient. And by having seven men living in one cabin, the guys could save lots of rent money!

Being on a shoestring budget and being short on culinary skills, the single guys worked out a deal with the single staff women at CRU headquarters to come up to the cabin once a week to cook a meal. The wrestlers bought the food and the single ladies prepared a nice home-cooked dinner. This arrangement would last during October and November, before the AIA wrestling tour started. It was also their version of *The Dating Game*—single men meeting single women at a nice dinner in a Christian environment. Gene Davis—the married guy—was there to keep the single wrestlers (Larry Amundson, John Hansen, John Klein, Loren Miller, Mitsuo Nakai, and Doug Smith) cultured enough to mingle with the single ladies. Such a good arrangement! Well, so everyone thought.

The result was a clash of gender and cultural differences from the beginning. Picture these sweet, nice, attractive women (who were looking for mature men of God), refined in the art of providing a lovely dinner as they served seven hungry and thirsty wrestlers coming home after a long, tough workout. This mountain cabin bachelor pad was more like a Christianized *Animal House*! For instance, at one of the first dinners a wrestler said, "Pass the butter" to his teammate at the opposite end of the table. His buddy literally passed the stick of butter and the butter plate with the finesse of an all-star quarterback. As it whisked past the refined secretary's face, the butter and the plate separated. While the receiving wrestler made a spectacular catch of the plate, the butter hit the "bull's-eye" into his glass of milk! That was just the beginning of many "romantic" dinners in the Christianized *Animal House*. The single ladies from Arrowhead Springs headquarters would never be the same, and the reputation of the new AIA wrestling team single guys spread like a prairie fire!

Finances continued to be an issue at the cabin. Gene, John, and Loren grew up hunting. Having not raised their full financial support, they were looking for creative ways to survive. Hunger became a primal force, especially after their tough workouts. Creativity was needed! Why not go into the woods and look for free venison walking on the hoof? A rumor was spread quickly that a deer wandered into their yard and died of a sudden heart attack. Although the story was suspect, the venison was delicious. They invited all the single women from CRU headquarters to dine along with their married wrestling teammates, whose wives were really impressed with the meal. More than forty people showed up for the feast, including visiting wrestlers from the touring Japanese Olympic team. Needless to say, it was a very large deer.

Numerous unplanned events happened at the single men's mountain cabin that bonded the new teammates. Doug Smith came up the driveway one day from an errand, jumped out of his car to walk into the cabin, and his car started rolling down the hill toward a creek. Being a strong wrestler, he tried to stop the car from rolling. As the car dragged Doug over the creek bank, he clung to the bumper with his heels dug four-inches deep into the dirt.

His last words before going out of sight were, "I know I pulled the emergency brake up. I know I did!"

One of the guys was a bug collector in his childhood days. One morning he spotted a giant prized tarantula. He gassed it and preserved the creature by displaying it on a block of wood with a pin stuck through its huge black torso. To him it was a magnificent specimen—a thing of beauty.

Later that day after a stop at the Orange Julius shop, the wrestlers walked in from their workout, and there on the dining room table was the trophy, the newly captured tarantula. The first wrestler to spot it screamed out, and in a fit of self-protection quickly took off his shoe and beat the living daylights out of the big spider, its body parts flying everywhere. The prized magnificent specimen had to be vacuumed up piece by piece off the floor!

There are many more stories, too numerous to mention (or even be allowed to mention). Suffice it to say there was never a dull moment in the mountain cabin where the single guys lived. Mercifully, the team never rented the cabin again. But their adventures were just beginning.

Meanwhile, down in the hot and smoggy San Bernardino Valley, the three married men tried to settle down and keep their wives happy on this new venture. Bob and Janet Anderson, Greg and Sue Hicks, and Doug and Jackie Rickard tried to settle into their new normal. These women had agreed to give up their lives, their goals, and their plans for the future, all for the sake of their husbands' dreams to use their wrestling talents to represent Christ to fans around the United States. "For better or for worse" came literally true for these young wives!

The wrestlers themselves were not sure where this idea of the AIA wrestling team was eventually headed, but their wives supported them 100 percent. One thing the wives fully agreed on was that God was up to something very unique, no matter how difficult it was for them to see the vision in a clear way during the early days. The thought of traveling for four months on the road and living with strangers near each college campus on the schedule was not their idea of keeping house. But for now they were willing to give it a chance. After all, they also had been taught at CRU staff training on how to speak to women's sororities, women's athletic teams, and at women's dormitory meetings on campus. They even formed a singing group, led by Pat's wife, Carrie, so they could include songs in their presentations to women's groups whenever possible. While their husbands were practicing and wrestling, Janet Anderson, Frances Davis, Sue Hicks, and Jackie Rickard were preparing to share Christ with others. The wives very quickly became an integral part of the AIA team.

The wives also sacrificed enormously—even more than the men. Living out of suitcases on a very low salary could not have been the life they had envisioned when they married the men they loved. But God drew them all to AIA wrestling, an unexpected detour in their marriage plans. Whether up front speaking or behind the scenes encouraging their husbands, they supported all the wrestlers faithfully through thick and thin.

Throughout the first summer and fall of 1968, this new team of young men and women were being molded by God into a force to be reckoned with both on and off the mat. The hardships they faced simply made the molding process happen faster than normal. Learning to live with each other confined in cars while traveling thousands of miles for four solid months was going to be difficult. Although they were essentially strangers just months earlier, the foundation was being laid and crafted by God's tough love, and the impact would be felt for decades. This team was ready to launch a ministry that no one was going to stop—ever.

As King Solomon said three thousand years earlier,
"Iron sharpens iron—so one man sharpens another."
(Proverbs 27:17)

Arrowhead Springs—International headquarters
in 1968 of CRU, parent organization of AIA.

Dave Hannah, AIA founder and director,
speaking at an athletic conference.

Arrowhead Springs Village, where the first AIA recruiting camp was held.

July 1968—The first AIA wrestling team family.

The wives singing group, 1968—Standing:
Janet Anderson, Carrie Matrisciana,
Jackie Rickard. Seated: pianist and AIA
administrator Gail Moore, and Sue Hicks.

Larry Amundson speaking to a crowd with
teammates and wives looking on.

First AIA wrestling team ready for the first tour against top college teams.

Chapter 4

The Travel Begins

It is the work that God does through us that
counts, not what we do for Him.
—Oswald Chambers

November 1968

It was with great anticipation as November 1968 rolled around for the new AIA team members. Richard Nixon had just been elected president; the Vietnam War protests were growing larger; the college campus radicals and the "peace through love" hippies were beginning to create chaos on and off college campuses across the United States. College campuses were becoming political hotbeds, and there was trouble in the streets as young people sought to "destroy the Establishment"—any traditional power structure such as government, campus authorities, and even parents.

Into this climate the first AIA wrestling team was about to launch its inaugural tour to tell college students about another revolutionary figure—Jesus, the Son of God. As a new believer, John Hansen would say to people who would listen, "It is not The Doors [the famous rock group] who 'lights my fire' but a new relationship with Christ that lights me up from within!"

A "warm-up match" for the big tour was scheduled against a group of Southern California College All-Stars. It was the one and only home match the AIA team would ever have, and they won handily!

The team created a new and unheard of event during the match. A "halftime" was created where the AIA wrestlers spoke to the audience about Christ. Never in history had a college wrestling match had a halftime like a basketball or football game.

AIA made history in more ways than one. People listened intently as the athletes spoke briefly about their personal faith and gave a short message of motivation for the audience to make a personal commitment to Christ. Comment cards were passed out to the crowd for a personal response—another first at a wrestling match. Attendees were asked to write their opinions on the cards and respond to the wrestlers' comments. Several people in the audience indicated they prayed to receive Christ. Amazing! People came to a wrestling match and two hours later walked out of the gym as a new believer in Christ. That was another first! AIA was plowing new ground while creating a bold new way to present the message of Christ.

The real athletic test came a short time later at a Division II college powerhouse, Cal Poly, in San Luis Obispo, California—a beautiful campus on rolling green hills. Cal Poly had finished sixth as a team at the Penn State Nationals. The gym was packed as the publicity attracted the media and many people curious to see the new AIA All-Star Wrestling Team meet the local heroes on the mat. AIA won the tough match 19–11 and spoke to well more than one thousand people about their faith in Christ.

The new team was off and running with a 2–0 start, not bad for a group of guys who twelve months earlier had never even met each other, nor had they heard the name Athletes in Action! The team was ready for their first extensive road trip and for a big test against number-one ranked University of Oklahoma and top-five ranked Oklahoma State in the same week. To get from Southern California to Norman, Oklahoma, seemed easy enough. Find I-40 and go east about twelve hundred miles! In 1968 it was find the old Route 66 along with a few completed parts of I-40 and go east, without cell phones and without a GPS, in a four-car caravan with ten wrestlers, three wives, and two children!

Transportation was a logistics nightmare. Doug and Jackie Rickard had a big green station wagon. (Picture the Griswold's car in the movie *National Lampoon's Vacation*.) To make it more exciting, the former rebellious student and new Christian teammate, John Hansen, was chosen to ride with the all-American family as their "sidekick." John became the designated babysitter for the Rickards' little boy, Brian. Larry, in his sparkling new Chevrolet Camaro, could only transport one other person, so Mitsuo rode with him. John Klein had Greg and Sue Hicks in his 1966 Oldsmobile Cutlass. All the others crammed into Bob and Janet Andersons' old VW bus, a relic from Bob's surfing days in Southern California. The cars lined up to form a caravan that lasted fewer than one hundred miles, and then it morphed into a competitive free-for-all to see who could get to Oklahoma first. The Great American Race was on!

After two long days and a short night of sleep, everyone found their way to Norman, Oklahoma, albeit at different times on the Wednesday before Thanksgiving. The last car finally arrived around four in the morning. Team leader Pat had left for Oklahoma a day earlier than the caravan to set up housing for the team. He had arranged for their home base to be an abandoned fraternity house near the OU campus. Pat planned to greet the team there. But when the first car arrived late at night, Pat was nowhere to be found. There was no key or instructions on how to get into the frat house—nothing! This was decades before cell phones.

What would any weary wrestler do with his team locked out? He would break into the house! Exhausted, everyone grabbed an empty room and tried to get some much-needed sleep. A few hours later a CRU staff member showed up and gave directions to drive into Oklahoma City for a Thanksgiving dinner with big supporters of the local CRU ministries. Pat finally showed up. A good meal was very welcomed after two days on the road. The wrestlers were cutting weight for the match weigh-in later, but it was Thanksgiving and everyone ate well! The old frat house became home for ten days as the team prepared for speaking engagements on the OU campus and the two big matches. The kitchen appliances worked well and everyone pitched in to cook meals on the fly. It was organized chaos for several days, but they were one big happy family.

Finally the anticipated match day with the University of Oklahoma arrived. OU had a loaded team! They were ranked number one in the nation's preseason polls after finishing third at Penn State. The match very quickly turned into a barn burner before the fifteen hundred fanatical wrestling fans at OU's Field House. Here's how the exhilarating evening evolved:

- The first match was a 1–1 draw. Mitsuo Nakai created a prelude for the night to come.
- John Hansen won in the 130-pound weight class.
- Doug Smith suffered a loss at 137 pounds.
- The 145-pound weight class wrestler Doug Rickard won.
- Loren Miller lost his 152-pound match in a heartbreaking 13–12.
- Greg Hicks lost 3–1 wrestling in the 160 lb class.
- Larry Amundson won his 177-pound class because of a twenty-second riding time advantage.

The score was now OU 14, AIA 11. It was up to Bob Anderson in the 190-pound class to salvage the match for Athletes in Action. Bob won the match in a gritty performance of 5–4 by a one-second riding time advantage to make the final team score 14–14. AIA's brand-new team tied the number-one ranked NCAA Division I team by a one-second riding time advantage!

Oklahoma University coach Tommy Evans said after the match, "I thought they were capable of beating us. It was a tough match to just sit there and watch." Coach Evans was one of the coaches willing to let his team wrestle AIA and allow team members to take a halftime in order to share their purpose—presenting Christ as a real solution to college students' personal lives. The program went off smoothly and comment cards were collected from the fans, after writing down their reaction to the team's presentation. The local CRU staff members followed up with the OU fans who wanted more information later on that week. Even more important than the match results, the team learned quickly that students loved hearing them speak. During the week the wrestlers spoke several times, particularly to the large "Greek" population on campus. The fraternities and sororities were excited to hear the AIA athletes since wrestling was such a popular sport in the state of Oklahoma. More than two thousand students heard Christ presented to them that week in Norman.

A few days later, the team drove eighty miles north to take on the Oklahoma State University Cowboys in Stillwater. Because of the team's tie match at OU, the days of surprising any team were over forever. Every college coach knew that grappling with the AIA boys would be a formidable task. Ironically, only two years after graduating from OSU, Gene Davis returned to coach against his former coach, Myron Roderick. However, due to an injury, Gene was unable to wrestle and compete against his former team. The Cowboys prevailed 20–8 with only Mitsuo and Loren winning their matches, along with John Klein's match ending in a 2–2 tie. But this outstanding event drew thirty-six hundred fans to Gallagher Hall, and all the fans heard the AIA team present the Good News of Christ. The crowd appreciated the quality wrestling competition and responded warmly to the halftime presentation.

For the team's first official big-time competitive trip, the time in Oklahoma set the tone for things to come. It was the beginning of an amazing strategy that lasted twenty years. The strategy was to schedule a big college match and spend several days on campus speaking to any group willing to listen to the athletes—sororities, fraternities, athletic teams, dorm groups, student associations, and in the classrooms! Eventually the strategy would be expanded to include churches, youth groups, FCA huddles, high schools, prisons, and civic clubs.

The last day at the OU frat house was a time for exchanging Christmas gifts (very inexpensive Christmas gifts) and singing around a three-foot-tall Christmas tree someone had purchased. After the team's party ended, it was time to split up and go home for a two-week break. But before the team left, there was some cleaning up to do at the frat house. Someone threw the Christmas tree into the huge fireplace and lit it. But they forgot to open the flue and thick dark smoke immediately filled the room. A fire alarm sounded and the firemen came quickly with sirens blaring. The last people the team shared Christ with in Norman, Oklahoma, were the local firemen! This was not a normal strategy to reach out to first responders, but the AIA teammates would talk to anyone who would engage in conversation.

As the team headed home for Christmas break, the men and wives were exhausted but excited and had a new confidence that this team was going to be the start of something special both on and off the mat. With a 2–1–1 record against very strong competition, the team's athletic strength was better than anticipated, especially considering they still had no practice facility, practice teammates, no home meets, and no hometown fans. It was the Christians versus the lions, at least in their minds. But the very unconventional team environment and the spiritual "warfare" just made the men work out that much harder. After all, they were all competing for a much higher cause.

It was also gratifying how many people had heard a clear practical message about Christ. In just more than a month of traveling, the team had spoken to almost seven thousand people in different settings—both athletic and social, on and off campus. And everyone listened attentively to these great athletes just as Dr. Bill Bright, Dave Hannah, Pat Matrisciana, and John Klein had suspected they would.

After a well-deserved Christmas break, the team took off on a Western United States swing in January 1969. Possibly because of overconfidence the team stumbled and lost their first match to the Oregon State Beavers in Corvallis, Oregon. Here for the first time the team encountered negative feedback regarding their presentation of the message of Christ. Their coach had some unkind words with John Klein and Gene Davis after the match. This marked the beginning of a persistent legal and political tug of war of whether the message of Christ would be allowed in the college arenas in the United States by a visiting athletic team.

With the setback at Oregon State, the team regrouped and then reeled off eight straight wins and won eleven of their twelve matches against Oregon, Colorado, Washington, Iowa State, UCLA (AIA winning 33–0), and Northwestern. Several AIA guys wrestled against their alma maters: Doug Richard at Colorado State College; Doug Smith at the University of Washington; and Bob Anderson at Adams State. All won at their home arena!

Near the end of the first season the team had scheduled a small college, Northwest Missouri State University, which had a great wrestling program. Head coach Gary Collins had attended the first AIA recruiting camp in San Bernardino, along with two of his college wrestlers. Coach Collins knew there was no CRU staff on their campus to follow up with interested people in learning more about Christ. If the AIA team would come, he agreed to personally help with the follow-up. He even organized and promoted the match, plus arranged several speaking engagements for the team to receive donations to help pay for their trip to Missouri. The AIA team discussed if they should go to a small campus with no local full-time CRU staff, but they accepted the challenge and headed to the Northwest Missouri State University campus.

Was the AIA team ever surprised! There were two thousand excited fans in the packed gym to see the dual meet. The whole town was excited to see their local boys go against the AIA All-Stars. At the previous match at Iowa State, two of the AIA wrestlers were injured. So the team was down 12–0 before the match started—due to two forfeits. The match was a rousing success with the AIA team barely winning over Northwest Missouri State. The fans embraced the half-time presentation and the comment card responses were overwhelmingly positive. Their coach was elated! And a critical lesson was learned by the AIA teammates that night. God can create the greatest spiritual results in the smallest, least-likely place!

Just before the final match of the initial season with Southern Illinois, Gene Davis and Greg Hicks were invited to New York City to try out for the US National Team heading to the World Wrestling Championships. Although US folk-style wrestling has different rules than Freestyle or Greco-Roman (all upper body technique) wrestling in the rest of the world, Gene and Greg went to the team's trials and tested their mettle. There was some small success even though neither of them made the US team. That trip opened up a door to the global sphere of sports, and God would use it mightily in the years to come, putting AIA athletes on the world stage. Whether it was the world stage, New York City, or a little college town in northwest Missouri, it did not matter. God was going to clearly use this team to His ultimate glory! The team's first wrestling season was complete and successful. What would the next season bring? Would everyone stay with the team for another year?

"A man's gift makes room for him and
brings him before great men."
(Proverbs 18:16)

Chapter 5

Four Years and Multiplied Thousands

If you ever had a vision of God, you may try as you like to
be satisfied on a lower level, but God will never let you.
—Oswald Chambers

1968–72

Normally a student goes to college for four to five years to earn a degree. At least that's the plan. A lot can happen in four to five years! No one could have possibly known how far things would go and what God was going to do with the AIA wrestling team from the sketchy, shaky first days in 1968 through the 1971–72 wrestling season. For the second wrestling season in the fall of 1969, John Klein was officially named team director as the team prepared for the new challenges ahead.

Between the summers of 1968 and 1972, American society was unraveling. Social upheaval was everywhere. College buildings were being burned to the ground by angry anti-establishment college students. Thousands of young men were dying in the Vietnam War. And in the midst of the cultural and social revolution, there were Athletes in Action athletic teams going boldly into some of the most heathen places in the United States—college campuses—proclaiming Jesus of Nazareth as the real revolutionary!

There is an old saying in Christian circles: "God doesn't want your ability, He wants your availability!" In the case of the wrestlers and their wives, God used both their ability and availability. They had tremendous athletic talent, and they relentlessly honed their skills to represent the cause of Christ as champions. They also worked diligently on the other skills necessary to help fulfill their calling. Namely they became excellent speakers and communicators of their central message, that a personal relationship with Christ could change everything by bringing peace and forgiveness into a person's life. Along with hundreds of CRU staff members each summer, the wrestlers and their wives learned more about the Bible and honed their ministry skills. As they grew in spiritual maturity, they became proficient in sharing their faith and efficient in counseling others. The more committed they became athletically and spiritually, the more God blessed and used them. "Whatever your hand finds to do, do it with all your might" (Ecclesiastes 9:10).

These men and women in their early twenties were becoming pioneers, plowing new ground, planting seeds, making mistakes, yet seeing profound results in the fruits of their labor—many times in places where the message of Christ was rarely or never heard. Jesus said in Matthew 28:18–19, "All authority has been given to me in heaven and on earth … therefore go!" The wrestlers were fully committed to *go* after the first summer.

From the start, the team sensed the power of their message. The response from the audiences in written form was highly motivational each time the athletes spoke. The impact of their message was swift, immediate, and measurable. Each person in the audience was handed a comment card and asked to give an honest opinion of the wrestler's message, no matter the setting. Most people responded. Because of this, a substantial written record was generated of what people thought and how they were affected. The team wanted a measure of how their message impacted people plus wanted to send information about Christ to anyone who asked for help. If the local CRU people were available to follow up with interested people, their names were given to them for personal contact. Very surprising were the honest and open comments from many people who felt free to reveal their inner feelings and personal problems or anxieties. Often the responses included heartfelt revelations of personal issues and of how God would be the answer to their needs and inner desperation.

Here are some samples of revealing comments handed in to the wrestlers.

"I thought the program was very beautiful. It gave me a feeling I can't quite describe when you guys talked about your acceptance of Christ."

"The program made me think there is something missing in my life."

"As I try to write, I find my mind quite blank—I'm impressed in a way I can't explain."

"I have been trying to figure out my life for a couple months and it has given me a new perspective to the whole situation. Thank you! Yes, I did accept Christ to control my life."

Along the way, there were times things happened to the team that no one could simply make up ... bizarre and funny things. In the dead of a very cold and snowy winter, the AIA team was on tour to wrestle at the University of Minnesota, a Big Ten powerhouse. The team was invited to dinner at the home of a distinguished professor of biblical archaeology at nearby Bethel College in St. Paul. After constant traveling on the road and a tough afternoon practice, the guys and their wives met at the professor's lovely home to enjoy a good home-cooked meal beautifully prepared by his gracious wife.

When the team arrived there was lots of hustle and bustle to feed the fifteen people, so the AIA wives jumped in to help. Finally everything was ready. All they needed was to say the blessing and the hungry wrestlers could enjoy the feast. Jackie Rickard was asked by the professor's wife to light the candles on the buffet, which were positioned precariously near the dining room curtains. As everyone bowed their heads, popping noises were suddenly heard, and everyone felt heat! The curtains were on fire! Screams for water went up as everyone scattered, raising havoc in the dining room. Quick minds and quicker hands prevailed as the fire was snuffed out before much damage was done. The scorched curtains hung pitifully from the curtain rods.

After the adrenalin rush, everyone settled down for the meal with the strong scent of smoke filling the air. Then the host couple had a real surprise. Their basement was full of artifacts from Israel and Palestine brought home from their travels—mementos of their treasured archaeological discoveries. The hosts were so excited; they pulled out their slide projector and turned down the lights to share their travels with the team.

Sometimes wrestlers can be … well, wrestlers. Once the lights were dimmed, John Hansen and Larry Amundson fell asleep lying on the carpeted floor while watching the slides. They'd had a long practice and the environment was ideal for a quick nap. They were so comfortable they started snoring—loudly. Fellow teammates continually kicked them to keep them awake for the remainder of the slide show. The professor simply ignored the distractions as if he were lecturing a class at the university. Academics and athletics sometimes uncomfortably coexist.

Often the team affected people without even being conscious of it. The team was invited to a hamburger cookout by a Christian family in Southern California. The family also invited their neighbors to join in the fun. The team showed up, ate heartily, and goofed around with each other—teasing each other relentlessly. After the great meal, Bob Anderson struck up a conversation with one of the neighbors at the kitchen table and suddenly was sharing a booklet "The Four Spiritual Laws." This was CRU's short and simple booklet with the message of how a person could begin to have a personal relationship with Christ.

When Bob had finished reading through the booklet with the neighbor, he asked his new friend if he wanted to accept Christ into his life. The man said yes. They then prayed together at the kitchen table.

When Bob asked why he felt he had a need for Christ in his life, the gentleman said, "I have never been around a group of people who obviously loved each other so much. There must be something to it!"

The wrestlers were just being guys who happened to love Christ fully and loved each other unconditionally.

One of the inevitable results of Christians actively sharing their faith is that the impact begins to multiply. In those first four years the team had spoken to approximately fifty thousand people every year. People were paying attention, and hundreds were coming to a newfound faith in Christ. And thousands of Christians heard the team as well and were strongly affected by the utter boldness of these wrestlers. Many believers responded to the team by saying the wrestlers challenged them to fully return to Christ in their own lives.

Note the following comments written by Christian students:

"I loved your presentation. I've been a Christian for four months and never met any athletes who were Christian."

"As a Christian, this was one of the finest presentations I ever witnessed. A lot of people can identify with AIA."

"Tonight I asked Him to return and regain control of my life."

These fearless athletes and their wives would speak about Christ anytime and anywhere. To them it became as natural as breathing. It was their passion that attracted attention, and therefore when they spoke, people responded both negatively or positively. Their lives were genuine and people could not be neutral after hearing their challenging message. Their message almost demanded a response!

In the spring of 1969 the University of California in Berkeley was ablaze with multiple demonstrations and chaos. The campus and Telegraph Avenue were full of radical militant students, professors, and outright communists. Berkeley's campus radicals spearheaded the war to bring down America's "Establishment." Soon other college campuses in the United States were following their lead with free-speech platforms and marching in the streets. Just a few miles away in San Francisco, the Haight-Ashbury district had become the unofficial headquarters for the hippie's free love and peace movement. This pocket of the country was leading the way for "revolution" and change through rebellion and violence.

Pat Matrisciana and his wife, Carrie, decided this would be the perfect place for some of the young wrestlers and their wives to have an "off-season excursion." The mission for John Klein, Greg and Sue Hicks, and Gene and Frances Davis was to share Christ to these rebellious crowds and to challenge the radicals' thinking. The first assignment was to look grubby with no shaving allowed, and wearing "flower child" clothes in order to blend in with the people in Berkeley. The second assignment was to join the massive street demonstrations so they could talk to students about The Great Revolutionary—Jesus! They went to the "free-speech platform" armed with the leaflet "Jesus and the Intellectual," written by a Christian college professor—a leader in the soon-to-be "Jesus movement." The wrestlers and their wives gave out hundreds of leaflets and talked to any student who would engage them in conversation. It was an odd fit for the athletes—all-American kids sharing Christ with anti-American kids. Surprisingly, many Berkeley students listened with intensity and engaged in debate.

One night the AIA folks attended a massive planning meeting for "The People's Park Riot"—a street demonstration to force the UC Berkeley board of directors to turn over a small park to the students. The leaders of every major radical group were allowed to speak on the stage. The Black Panthers wanted to hide guns under their girlfriends' dresses. Leaders from the SDS (Students for a Democratic Society) wanted to hold a massive march, attack the police, and burn buildings.

It was clear from this meeting that the radical movement was being orchestrated by older leaders who were not students. These leaders used idealistic students to advance the movement and their mission to change the American system and its structure. Media outlets did a poor job reporting the whole truth. Exaggeration was rampant in the media, and no one seemed to know what was really going on with the various radical groups. The leaders were deadly serious that violence against innocent people and destruction of property were part of the master plan to bring down the governing authorities.

Although the wrestlers and their wives impacted a few people in Berkeley, their experience taught them several lessons:

1) How to evade the police and the National Guard, who were goaded into arresting the people they could chase down. The police and National Guard would ask a few questions and marchers immediately were hauled off to jail.
2) How idealistic people can be misled by evil and mass manipulation in a mob environment.
3) How real enemies of the American way of life want to destroy cherished freedom and liberty, including religious freedom.

A cultural war was on and gaining momentum! The Berkeley experience was very worthwhile.

After the first successful year, the team's first key decision in the summer of 1969 was to relocate to a more central geographic location in Oklahoma City, Oklahoma, from California. It was a state that loved the sport of wrestling, and Oklahomans welcomed the team with open arms.

Moving the team from Southern California to Oklahoma City was no small feat. Every AIA wrestler and family had to move; the office equipment had to be moved; everything was uprooted. The administrative assistant, Faith Bode, had to move as well. Faith was the only single woman on the team.

Nothing was simple when moving a whole team. To save money they rented a U-Haul truck. Gene, Frances, Larry, and Faith gathered all the team's equipment, packed it on the truck, and started the long journey. Gene was notorious for never checking his gas gauge, and the truck soon ran out of gas in the middle of the Arizona desert.

Larry and Gene drove Faith's car about ten miles until they saw a house. They borrowed a gallon of gas that was poured into an empty plastic milk bottle. The kind homeowner said, "Whatever you do, please bring back the bottle." Larry promised.

When Larry and Gene got back to the truck, Gene poured most of the gas into the tank. But he decided to pour a little gas down the carburetor to help jump start the gas-depleted truck. When Larry turned the key—POOF—a loud noise and huge spark flashed out of the carburetor and caught the plastic bottle on fire. Thinking fast, Gene threw the ignited bottle on the ground, and the parched grass caught fire! The bottle melted into a big hot ball of plastic. In stark panic, the four of them fought the grass fire furiously with water and U-Haul blankets.

Standing in the aftermath with smoke slowly rising from the extinguished fire, they looked at each other and made an executive decision. They would head toward Oklahoma City as soon as they could while asking God to forgive them for the bottle turning into a melted ball of plastic, and for never going back to explain themselves to the bottle's owner.

An added bonus for moving the team to Oklahoma City was that the Oklahoma State and the University of Oklahoma head coaches allowed the AIA team to divide up team members and work out with their respective teams once a week. The other four days of the week workouts were spent in a borrowed church gym in Oklahoma City. This was an unusually low profile workout facility for such a highly successful team!

Every day these wrestlers rolled out the mats on the gym floor and taped them down. They worked out hard and then mopped the mats clean and stowed them away. The team, however, did not seem to notice the irony, because wrestlers are used to improvising. This team, which was loaded with many great nationally recognized athletes, was mopping its own mats, washing its own workout gear, and eating hot dogs instead of steak. Team members were turning down salaried jobs to raise their own financial support. They had no team trainers, no whirlpool, and few medical supplies, but it simply did not matter to these guys. God honored their humility.

New teammates were added to the Oklahoma City team each year. As is the tradition in athletics, these starry-eyed rookies wanted to impress the veteran wrestlers in any way possible.

First-year wrestler Brian Dameier, a New Orleans native and a recruit from LSU, tells his story:

> We were practicing at a gym on the campus of Nichols Hills Baptist Church. Because wrestling was our main exercise, we often played soccer or basketball to break up our routine. There is a different set of rules when wrestlers play basketball and it can get rough. One of our veteran wrestlers went down with a badly sprained ankle, and we thought a doctor should look at it. Without thinking, I volunteered to drive and got the keys to Reid Lamphere's car. Outside it had snowed about two inches. As teammates got our injured wrestler into the car, I gunned it and took off heading for the hospital. The car did a full 360-degree circle in the church parking lot, spinning through the snow like a NASCAR winner's celebratory doughnut burnout at the end of a race. I took my foot off the gas and floored it again—another 360-degree spinout! Then it hit me—I'm from New Orleans and I have never even seen snow, much less driven in it. I ran back in the gym and shouted, "I've never driven on snow! Can someone else drive?"

The injured veteran wrestler still lying in the back seat was not only dizzy but wondering if he was going to be more seriously injured just trying to get out of the parking lot!

By the second and third wrestling seasons, more and more college wrestlers were taking notice of the tough AIA boys and their message of "revolution." Sometimes after competing against the AIA grapplers, a college wrestler would believe in Christ.

Here are two letters received from college wrestlers who were led to Christ because of the AIA team being on their campus:

"I am finally getting around to writing you. I've been doing remarkably well this year in school and wrestling. It must be my new belief in Christ. Sometimes when I'm in a rut, my belief in Christ and the Christian way helps me get out of it. I thank you for showing me the way!"

"Sorry that I have postponed this letter, but I've had lots of mid-semester tests. I have been doing a lot of thinking about your suggestions. I believe I have finally accepted Jesus to guide my life, for He is the only way! As I look around the world it seems the only people who have inner peace are those who have a personal relationship with Christ. Through your inspiration I have asked Christ into my life. When I start to feel down about something, Christ comforts me. Thank you very much."

Several collegiate wrestlers felt the tug in their heart and joined AIA upon graduation. For example, Greg Hicks led Jim Axtell to Christ at wrestling practice at Minnesota. Doug Smith led Bill Gifford to Christ at Springfield College, Massachusetts. Eddie Rew influenced Minnesota's All-American Mike McArthur to come to Christ. The AIA team began to reproduce itself!

Dan Moskowitz, a wrestler from a Jewish background, tells his story:

> The AIA wrestling team was invited to do a presentation at American University. One of my university wrestling teammates, who was a Christian, had been pursuing me relentlessly for several months and even gave me the AIA magazine to read. The AIA wrestlers who presented were Bob Kuhn, Sam Hieronymus, Dick Pollack, and Steve Gaydosh. I remember Sam sharing his testimony, and I also remember someone reading a quote from the Bible where Jesus says, "Behold, I stand at the door and knock: if anyone hears my voice and opens the door, I will come in to them." I thought, *That sounds like a challenging statement.* I figured if Jesus was who He said He was, He would come in and somehow I would know it. So when they prayed, I joined in. Something changed in me at that moment—I just knew that I knew. I was as sure of His reality as I had ever been of anything before or since. I

was really excited and filled out a comment card. In my excitement, I forgot to check the "I received Jesus" box on the card. I learned later that my friend who had invited me looked over to see if I had checked the box. He was crushed to see that I had not, but he could not read what I had written on the card. A few days later after practice, my Christian teammate and I were walking to dinner and he asked me if I had received Jesus. I said yes. He went crazy whooping and hollering and then bear-hugged me and threw me into a hedge of thorn bushes. Thus began my early training that to be counted with Christ, you should expect to suffer.

The large crowds and big events, plus talking individually with fellow athletes were all exciting experiences, but meeting with regular individuals one on one was the most gratifying experience for them. Prior to the 1970 wrestling season, Reverend E. V. Hill invited CRU staff members to the Watts neighborhood in Los Angeles. He spoke at Arrowhead Springs and said his neighborhood had seen plenty of pimps and drug dealers come in but few Christians from the outside. His neighborhood had experienced serious racial unrest. CRU staff members, who at the time were predominantly Caucasian, were invited to go into the neighborhoods, house to house, to talk to people about their faith and then go to churches within the primarily African American community. Several wrestlers and wives were involved. Sue Hicks had a great conversation about Jesus with a fourteen-year-old girl in Watts. What an image during heightened racial tension. Imagine observing a young white woman from Greensboro, North Carolina—where the first black sit-in at an all-white lunch counter took place only a few years earlier— talking to a young black girl on her front porch in Watts. Only God can arrange such a meeting! The truth and love of Christ can melt racial prejudice if only people would listen to the message and then believe it.

A few days later a letter was received at CRU Headquarters asking for assistance:

"Dear Sir,

Saturday some of your Campus Crusade for Christ people came around to my neighborhood. They were: very nice and they explained to me what it is to be a good Christian. And I think that I got something out of it. I am fourteen years old and I think that if more young people could explain the word of God as the two young people did to me, I think more young people would believe in God. So can you send me some information on Campus Crusade for Christ International?"

By the fourth season many wrestlers had joined the team in Oklahoma City upon graduation from college. They were:

Jim Axtell, Minnesota

Nick Carollo, Adams State

Brian Dameier, LSU

Art Holden, Wisconsin-Whitewater

Reid Lamphere, Minnesota

John Lightner, Oklahoma State

Gary Rushing, Arizona

Henry Shaffer, Clarion State

Tom Talbert, Maryland

Gary Wallman, Iowa State

Kent Kershner, Montana State

John Hart, West Chester State

With additional teammates and less travel time on the road, their athletic toughness grew. In its third season (1970–71) the team sported a 13–1 record in dual meets and won the National Wrestling Federation Freestyle Championship with only thirteen wrestlers! Second place went to the New York Athletic Club with more than twenty team members. Until then there were only a few serious post-college amateur wrestling clubs in the United States, and the two clubs that dominated the team national championship trophy each year were the Mayor Daley Club out of Chicago and the New York Athletic Club. Both clubs recruited top post-college wrestlers who wanted to extend their careers in the freestyle wrestling competition so they could try out for the World Championship, Pan American, and Olympic teams. Suddenly the upstart AIA team showed up and won the first-place team trophy! And they did it with quality, not quantity. Three years earlier no one had ever heard of Athletes in Action, but now, as the National Freestyle Champs, everyone in the wrestling world took notice. This meant even more doors would start opening for the team around the world. This topnotch championship team was exhibit number one that Christians were not wimps!

> "I know your deeds. Behold, I have put before
> you an open door which no one can shut,
> because you have a little power, and have kept
> My word, and have not denied My name."
> (Revelation 3:8)

Chapter 6

A Pivotal Time from Oklahoma to Pennsylvania to Munich, Germany

God is not after perfecting me to be a specimen in His
showroom; He is getting me to the place where He can use me.
—Oswald Chambers

1972

After traveling thousands of miles by car and speaking to upwards of two hundred thousand people over four years, the National Freestyle Champion Team was on a roll! Their record against all competition was 36–7–1. The average attendance of the AIA matches was 1,231 fans. The team not only spoke in large arenas on campuses and to college athletic teams but to multiple venues in dozens of states and Canada. Hundreds of people had given their lives to Christ as a result. Former competitors were joining the AIA team every year after graduating from college, and the team continued to prosper.

Following the 1971 regular season and tournament championship, several AIA wrestlers were invited to try out for the US National Team for the upcoming World Championships in Sophia, Bulgaria. Gene Davis made the team in the 136.5-pound class. Greg Hicks, who got knocked out cold in a tryout match, was invited to be on the traveling team as an alternate at 180.5 pounds. The US borders were no longer going to be a geographical boundary for the AIA team! Gene and Greg knew Bulgaria was a puppet state of Russia, so they promptly ordered eighty Russian-language Bibles to quietly take across the Bulgarian border, stuffing them inside their athletic duffle bags.

When Gene and Greg landed in Sophia with the US team, a little nervousness stirred within them as their plane pulled up to the terminal. The team's bags were laid out on the tarmac in a long row as they formed a line for security guards to inspect each wrestler's bag. Gene and Greg felt a lump in their throats as they moved to the back of the line and started praying. Suddenly a Bulgarian tournament official ran up and yelled at the guards. Quickly they motioned for the entire team to go to the awaiting buses. There was no need to check the bags; they were athletes! Relax! God is in control, even in communist countries.

With their "contraband" in hand, Gene and Greg made it to the team hotel in a local athletic training facility. The US team members were assigned rooms on the top floor—the thirteenth floor of the Diana Hotel. They first thought their designated rooms were a special treat for the team to enjoy the great view of Sophia. Quickly they realized the elevator only worked half the time. This meant walking up thirteen floors after long practice sessions every day and back down for a meal later. The Communist officials were not stupid.

One thing that was ironic: the first day in Sophia at the training facility, the US team heard music over the loudspeaker. It was Ray Charles singing "Georgia on My Mind" at the nearby Olympic team pool. It is a fact that music and athletics are universal and cross all cultural divides.

Gene and Greg would work out with the team, shower, and then walk down the streets of Sophia, handing Russian-language Bibles to anyone who would take them. Most of the interested people were students—many who spoke broken English. Most had never seen an American. No one had ever seen a real Bible. Many took the Bible and looked around in fear as they stuffed it in their pocket or in a bag.

Having been duped or intimidated by the Communist propaganda machine, some simply handed the Bible back with a stone-faced glare. After all, it was illegal to have a Bible in the atheist culture of the Soviet Union, and there were snitches everywhere in case someone got out of line. One could go to jail for having a Bible in a Soviet state.

Fear and intimidation were ever-present in Bulgaria. People would constantly look around when talking to Gene and Greg, especially at the sight of the Bible. Even if these people did not read this Bible, many people took one because they could sell it on the black market for what was equivalent of a month's wages. One way or another the priceless book of Scriptures would make its way to a believer somewhere in the communist world and it would be cherished like gold. AIA wrestlers were spreading the "spiritual gold" over the world—even behind the Iron Curtain!

God opened up opportunities to share their faith in the busy city. Greg and Gene were trying to find a restroom, and in the Slavic language they could not even guess how to say "restroom" or how to find one. They entered a hotel bar knowing a restroom would be there.

A young Sophia University man said, in English, "Hello, the restroom is down this way." He introduced himself as Christopher and ordered lemonades for them while he quietly slid over toward the Americans. He was friendly and smiling as he spoke to them in perfect English.

When Christopher realized he had befriended two American wrestlers who were competing in the World Championship, he was elated. He was honest and spoke openly with no fear in his voice. He shared everything. His wife was forced to work in another city while he finished college in Sophia. The students of the Communist Party members always received As on their class grades. He secretly listened to the BBC or Voice of America for news.

He said, "I read our papers just to get the date." He shared that he loved reading about America and could not get uncensored books in English. Greg and Gene gladly gave Christopher an English Bible and Christian literature of all kinds from their backpacks.

They explained to him how Christ had changed their lives as Christopher listened intently. Christopher even had the courage to take Greg and Gene to his apartment. It was a sparse, single room with a bed, couch, kitchen table, and chairs. No TV was in sight. They talked for a half-hour as Christopher poured out his frustrations about the government controls and lack of freedom. He had many questions about America and freedom in general.

Then suddenly there was a knock at the door. Christopher turned glum and looked at us with a look of fear. His face pale, he stood up to open the door.

An older man walked in and started speaking in Bulgarian. Christopher exchanged a few words with him and then introduced his new wrestler friends. After about five minutes of discussion, the man left.

Christopher sat down again and told them the man was his landlord, who wanted to know all about these new guests in the apartment. He explained that they were wrestlers who were getting ready to compete in the big soccer stadium for the World Championships. The danger of course was that the landlord would turn Christopher in to the authorities for meeting with Americans and bringing them to his apartment. If they were to search the place, he would be in trouble for having a Bible and other Christian literature.

Christopher stood up and thanked them for meeting with him, but his joy was gone. Greg and Gene walked out thanking God that America was their home and still the land of the free and the brave. They committed to pray for Christopher and his safety.

The last thing Christopher said to them was (referring to Bulgaria), "I live in a prison—two hundred miles by three hundred miles. To me America is another planet!"

The World Games Tournament was held in the national soccer stadium with twenty to thirty thousand people attending each session. Every single match was on national TV. Wrestling legend

Dan Gable won his first World Championship gold medal for the US team. After the championships, Gene and Greg flew with the team to Communist East Germany, crossed through the Berlin Wall on the team bus, and then toured West Germany competing against local German clubs. The contrast was so stark from East Germany to West Germany, from fear in Eastern Europe to freedom in Western Europe. The impact of the trip was strong on Gene and Greg. They would never again take their freedom for granted. A fire was lit in their souls to travel abroad again and reach out as often as possible to the people like Christopher, who were trapped under the USSR's oppressive atheistic rule. And this they would do again and again!

By the fourth year, the AIA team was highly visible and respected in the wrestling world. College coaches were very interested in having the team visit their campuses and wrestle against their teams. More than one college coach quipped, "The AIA team comes to town and beats the hell out of your team and then tells them about the love of God." Not exactly theologically correct, but pretty close! The team members were more mature and polished from the constant travel and their experiences across North America. Keeping physically fit was nearly impossible with their schedules and they had to keep spiritually fit while engaging continually in the spiritual battle on the "front lines."

Not everyone responded positively to their message. One student wrote on a comment card, "Nausea set in on me—hypocrisy." Another wrote, "I want to go to hell, but I'm going to have a good time on earth." Still another bragged, "Dope is the answer." But these types of responses were few and far between.

The 1971–72 wrestling season opened with the Southern Open Tournament in Chattanooga, Tennessee, against great national competitors. The Thanksgiving weekend tournament drew top wrestlers from Oklahoma State, Iowa State, and other great teams. The CRU high school staff loved AIA and hosted a big Thanksgiving dinner for the team. They had team members speaking all over Chattanooga and Lookout Mountain in high schools, civic clubs, and to athletic teams. The newspaper favorably covered the tournament and the AIA team. One year earlier at the Southern Open the big match of the tournament was a head-to-head battle between AIA's Gene Davis and Iowa State's Dan Gable. The match was a huge battle of former NCAA champions, with Gene taking down Gable to his back for a four-point move, but Gable eventually prevailed by a 9–4 score. In the summer of 1972 they would both be on the US Olympic team but in different weight classes. One college wrestling coach a few months after the tournament wrote in a letter to the AIA team, "I want to thank you for what you did. Since you spoke to my team, two of my wrestlers have really changed. They are involved in Bible studies and have affected the whole team." AIA had several men make it to the finals in their weight class at the Southern Open.

In January 1971 the team was able to wrestle on television for the first time and present its halftime program. The general manager of CBS affiliate WRAL-TV in Raleigh, North Carolina, loved what AIA was doing on college campuses, especially during such tumultuous times. The general manager's name was Jesse Helms, and years later he would become a North Carolina senator. Greg Hicks's former wrestling coach at NC State, Jerry Daniels, arranged a collegiate all-star team with competitors from NC State, Duke, East Carolina University, and UNC-Chapel Hill. The television match was videotaped in the studio and was televised the following Saturday afternoon. The halftime presentation, including an invitation to respond to Christ, was shown in full. A few days later the CBS affiliate in Greensboro, North Carolina, WFMY-TV, taped a second match against the all-stars and broadcast it later to thousands of sports fans in the viewing area.

Just after Christmas in 1970, several AIA team members traveled to Miami, Florida, for the Sunshine Open Wrestling Tournament. Tough wrestlers from Ohio, Oklahoma, and other colleges participated in the tournament and took in the warmer climate of south Florida. The tournament finals were held in a most unusual venue—on a dance floor at the Viking Steak House. The large restaurant had tables all around the dance floor and a second level balcony for eating. The finals were held while people ordered their dinners and chomped on prime rib. The competitors warmed up by the cooks in the kitchen alongside the pasta bar. The crowd loved it! The AIA team shared their halftime program with the fans and patrons about the purpose of the team. AIA had four champions at the tournament—and the post-match meal was extremely delicious and free to the finalists!

During the early years the team had many unusual circumstances in which to present their programs. One church had a father-son banquet, and the organizers wanted the team to demonstrate some wrestling techniques for the audience. So off to the nursery the AIA wrestlers went to get baby mattresses and sheets. Voila! The grapplers created makeshift mats to demonstrate their moves. Years later in Europe, the team did a wrestling clinic outdoors in a cow pasture. They picked a patch of tall grass and were careful to watch their step!

The AIA team wrestled Army at West Point in early 1972. What an honor to be on those hallowed grounds. On the day the team practiced with the Army team, the academy brass invited the AIA boys to eat in the mess hall with the four thousand cadets. The only problem was that two of the wives had traveled with the team, and women at that time were not allowed inside the mess hall. But somehow Ellen Amundson and Sue Hicks walked in with the AIA team and had a meal with the Corp of cadets. At the all-male academy, this was likely the first time that two women had ever eaten with the men in the mess hall. "Doors shall be opened!"

The summer of 1972 was to begin another milestone for the AIA team in more ways than one. The Olympic Games were being held in Munich, Germany. The German nation had truly come a long way in the twenty-six short years since World War II. Post-war Germany still had the Berlin Wall and was a divided country, with both East and West Germany.

But Munich wanted to become a showcase, with its gleaming new Olympic Stadium and subway system. AIA had several men trying out for the Olympic teams both in wrestling and weight lifting. Russ Knipp, of the AIA weightlifting team, made the squad, and Gene Davis secured a spot in the 136.5-pound weight class on the USA Olympic wrestling team.

AIA Wrestling initiated something else novel at the Munich Games with an Olympic outreach to the world's greatest athletes. Eight wrestlers and three wives decided to team up with the European CRU outreach team to concentrate primarily on the athletes in the Olympic Village, as well as the international sports fans. As usual everything was done on a shoestring budget. The team stayed in a private school with only a couple of showers, the men on one floor and women on the other. Fifty or so European students and CRU staff were housed there as well. Splash baths from the sink and sleeping bags on the floor were luxuries. The first ever Olympic outreach ran for two weeks. The Olympic outreach continues today, led by former AIA wrestler Reid Lamphere, who was at the Munich outreach.

The Olympic Village security was loose in 1972, and the wrestlers were able to get into the village just by wearing USA jackets and talking to the security guards. Talking with athletes from different countries was difficult with the language barrier, but materials and booklets were handed out whenever possible. It was the beginning of large international sports outreaches for the future.

And then the unthinkable happened. Arab terrorists broke into the village and took hostages from the Israeli Olympic team, including the wrestling coach and several wrestlers. The games came to a screeching halt! Lockdown and negotiations started. A poorly planned rescue operation at the Munich airport failed terribly. As a result, thirteen Israeli athletes and coaches were murdered, including a wrestler and wrestling coach. The world has never been the same. Olympic villages would never be opened to the public again, and virtual armies of security teams guard every Olympic venue today. The AIA folks and CRU team prayed diligently during those three dreadful days. Evil does exist, and it can be brutal! After the games reopened, AIA was part of a "Jesus march" through the streets of Munch with several hundred other Christians from many countries. They marched on the same streets that Hitler and his Nazi troops had marched just a quarter of a century earlier. What a sharp contrast between the evil of terror and the grace of Jesus.

On the mat, Gene Davis did not medal for his weight class, but two wrestling brothers, Ben and John Peterson, won a gold and a silver medal, respectively, for the United States. John would join the AIA East team the following year and later coach the east team.

By 1972 the oldest member of the AIA team was only twenty-nine years old. Every person on the AIA team roster was still in his twenties. The young men and their wives simply had a strong sense of mission, faith in God, and conviction to use their sport to reach the world for Christ. They dared believe God could lead them anywhere to influence anyone in the world through wrestling. Athletically, the sky was the limit! In these four short years, God did "above and beyond" what they ever expected, but there was even more to come. The world was becoming their mission field. Athletically they were strong, very successful, and respected by coaches, athletes, and sports fans worldwide. What would be next?

> "When a man's ways are pleasing to the Lord, He
> makes even his enemies to be at peace with him."
> (Proverbs 16:7)

Chapter 7

The Bridge So Wide

Spiritually we cannot measure our life by success
but only by what God pours through us.
—Oswald Chambers

1972–76

In 1967, when AIA recruiter Pat Matrisciana was walking and talking the "pipe dream" of creating a team of superb Christian wrestlers, he was not dreaming just within the nation's borders. In fact, Pat and AIA director Dave Hannah were dreaming much bigger—worldwide bigger. Visionary personalities tend to do that!

In one of Pat's recruiting letters in 1968, he challenged a recruit to join the new all-star team, saying they would tour the United States and "go to Bulgaria and Russia" in the first year. Pat turned out to be right about the countries but wrong about the date. Gene Davis and Greg Hicks made it to Bulgaria for the 1971 Wrestling World Championships. Greg and Mike McCready made it to the USSR in 1975 representing the United States in the world championships.

Interestingly, the Soviet Union's world championship team wrestled in the United States also in 1971. Several AIA wrestlers were chosen for the US national team during the Soviet team's US tour. It was the first dual meet between the USSR and the United States in years due to the political fallout of the Cold War. The Russians had come to AIA's shores first!

Flashing forward to today, there are AIA staff members in almost eighty countries, and in no small way the expansion came from the first international seeds planted in 1967 and 1968. How did the numbers grow from a few athletes in basketball and wrestling to eighty countries in fewer than forty-five years? It was not easy! The path looks disjointed and crooked, but God's invisible hand was always present. The wrestlers were instrumental in leading the growth, and they were the catalysts that made this expansion possible.

By the end of 1972 the team had grown so large that it split into two separate teams, doubling the potential speaking engagements and the number of matches against college wrestling teams each year. The west team was headquartered in Oklahoma City under team director Larry Amundson, and the new east team was headquartered in Lancaster, Pennsylvania, under team director Greg Hicks. Gene Davis continued to coach the west team while new head coach Neil Turner, former assistant coach at Clarion, led the east team. This expansion happened in a mere four years since of the AIA wrestling team commenced operations. Truly amazing things had happened so far. The teams would grow even larger over the next four years.

The reason Lancaster, Pennsylvania, was chosen in 1972 for the new AIA East wrestling team headquarters was because of a three-week AIA trip in January 1972. High school and collegiate wrestling is extremely popular in the Quaker state. All told, the team members spoke to approximately 14,000 people in forty-two engagements. Of the thousands of comment cards collected, 1,555 students indicated they made a personal commitment to Christ. One high school student wrote on her card, "While we were praying, I peeked around to see my friends with their heads bowed and I couldn't believe my eyes." A college sorority coed wrote, "I have never heard anything about having a personal relationship with Christ. I invited Christ into my life, and I want to get the materials to find where I go from here."

The Franklin and Marshall College assistant coach Stan Zeamer, who as a college freshman had attended the original AIA team recruiting team camp in 1968, opened the door for the new east team to use their wrestling room and gym for practice sessions. Again God used relationships to open doors. Stan later became head coach and became an ardent AIA wrestling promoter.

The west team remained in Oklahoma City but later decided to move to Long Beach, California, to take advantage of the massive population migration to the Pacific coast. They began to work out at Long Beach State because a friendly coach wanted the AIA team to be around his college athletes. For the next several years, the AIA West team competed in the west and Midwest, talking to thousands of people about Jesus Christ.

During the 1972–73 wrestling season, the west team's twelve wrestlers competed against thirteen college teams, going 11–2 for the season. The east team competed against college teams sixteen times all over the Eastern and Southern United States, with a record of 14–2.

By 1974–75 the Athletes in Action organization had grown rapidly. Along with east and west wrestling teams were east and west basketball teams, a touring weightlifting team, a small track team, and a gymnastics team. A professional sports division was rapidly expanding by providing sports chaplains in professional tennis, the NFL, Major League baseball, and on the PGA tour. AIA had its own television and radio department plus a sports publication division. They developed athletic Bible study materials and eventually broadcast AIA basketball games. AIA created "pro weeks" in cities using NFL players and AIA athletes to speak in dozens of high schools and churches and on college campuses and military bases. In a few short years, tens of thousands of people were reached in one-week outreaches in cities like Austin, Amarillo, Nashville, Indianapolis, and Birmingham. In some cities, the week culminated with a flag football game in a local stadium using NFL players who spoke at halftime about their faith. After the game they gladly signed autographs and wrote out their favorite Bible verses on game programs for hundreds of fans.

CRU, the parent of AIA sports ministry, had also made national headlines in 1972 with almost 90,000 people attending a training and outreach week called Expo '72 at the Cotton Bowl in Dallas, Texas. Billy Graham and other well-known Christian speakers spoke nightly as the AIA wrestlers and basketball players surrounded the stage as "security guards" for the event. The wrestlers' wives served as hostesses in the event speakers' green room near the big stage. CRU had grown to 4,344 staff members in dozens of countries, which would in a few years help AIA wrestlers launch ministry outreaches in other countries.

In the summer of 1974, Gene Davis, Greg Hicks, and heavyweight Mike McCready wrestled for the US team at the world championships in Istanbul, Turkey. Of the ten weight classes in the world championships, AIA represented three as members of the US National Team. After the 1972 Olympics, John Peterson joined AIA, allowing the team to have an Olympic silver medalist. John and Greg ironically wrestled in the same weight class at 82 kilograms (180.5 pounds) and met three straight years in the finals of the US National Freestyle Championships, with John winning two out of the three championships. They practiced together every day and then competed head to head in important tournaments and for US national teams!

As a matter of fact, for six consecutive years (1971–76), either John or Greg won the freestyle competition to represent the United States in the world championships and Olympic games in the 82-kilogram weight class, with John being a two-time Olympic medalist. During the same six-year period, Gene Davis and Mike McCready represented the 62-kilogram weight class (136 pounds) and the 100-plus-kilogram weight class (heavyweight) respectively, three times each. Team members owned the decade of the '70s in the international wrestling world for the US AIA National Team.

The AIA teams headed into the 1975–76 wrestling season feeling strong and confident that God would continue to open doors in many unique places and they could compete at the highest level. However, during the midseventies the political environment began to change in respect to the opportunities to continue speaking in high school assemblies, talking openly about Christ and often closing in prayer publicly. The ACLU and the threat of potential lawsuits were making school boards and school principals uneasy. As AIA teams became better known, colleges also started to say no to the AIA halftime presentations or anything of a spiritual nature, fearing a lawsuit or negative publicity. The secularization of America was steadily making its impact on society, eroding free-speech opportunities for the athletes.

The wrestlers, who were always improvising new strategies, decided to make creative adjustments and continue their programs regardless. The high school assemblies were incredibly popular with students. The assembly would begin with wrestlers demonstrating funny skits. For example, there was a weightlifting demonstration where a wrestler would pretend to get the barbell stuck on his nose as he struggled mightily to press the bar over his head. Then a wrestler would lie on his back and arch up into a neck bridge with just the top of his head and his two feet touching the mat, while the heaviest person in the crowd would be invited to come and stand on top of his stomach, demonstrating the amazing neck strength wrestlers possess. Then two of the wrestlers would show off their athleticism with flashy wrestling moves and high-flying throws. Finally the emcee would announce, "The goal of every athlete is to become a professional—and it is also true for every wrestler." The wrestlers would choose a popular athlete or teacher from the audience to be the "pro referee" and invite him to come to the mat. The wrestlers would joke around by doing hilarious wrestling tricks, such as exaggerated flips and pro-wrestling moves to the roaring laughter from the audience. Each AIA wrestler created his own pro wrestler character. Skunk Man and Evil Boll Weevil would tussle with Pig Farmer John and One Bum Knee. One Bum Knee was a South Korean wrestler named Kyung Mu Chang, who came to

America to share his faith in Christ with Americans with AIA. Talk about a missionary reversal!

Sandwiched between the funny skits, the wrestlers would share their personal stories about their sports careers and their relationships with Christ. Then they finished the assembly with an explanation of how each student and teacher could personally know Christ. Over the years, hundreds of thousands attended these assemblies. If allowed, the wrestlers would close the assembly with a prayer and collect personal comment cards for responses to the program.

The laughter and fun in the athletic environment created an atmosphere that opened the hearts of the students to listen to the message about Christ.

Once, after a high school assembly program, a letter was received from a student who was hurting inside. "I just came from an assembly held at our school. The assembly was given by four wrestlers from AIA, who gave a fine show of wrestling techniques. I enjoyed this part, but I can say that when they shared their experience with Jesus Christ with us, something changed in me. I have been attending a church for almost a year. I love the church and everything it is. I attend church twice a week and go through the motions. I sing the hymns and pray the prayers but knew something was missing, that there was something I had to know and feel before it could have meaning to me. And it's not just missing something in church; I was missing something in my whole life. It seemed that everything I did was wrong. I was called self-centered, conceited, and other little tidbits just as bad. I can't begin to explain how it felt but it wasn't a good feeling; it was tearing me apart. There was just no purpose of living. When those wrestlers started talking, I definitely started changing. I found there is a purpose in life and a reason for living—Jesus Christ, the most wonderful happening in my life. I want to thank the guys who brought about this change, and yes, I want to receive more information about AIA. Thank you, all."

As evidenced by this letter, individuals had real personal needs and issues they were trying to deal with every day. High school and college students particularly faced a harsh and cruel world, tremendous peer pressure, and a hedonistic culture that offered only a temporary or superficial solution to their inner needs. They were searching for real and reliable answers. Hundreds of comment card responses motivated the wrestlers to do whatever they could to get the message of God's love and forgiveness to the hurting students. The team intentionally and creatively worked hard to effectively present their message. Some critics considered their presentations edgy, too aggressive, or even offensive. Others resisted even before hearing them speak and pushed back against the team's presentations whenever they could.

In April 1976 *Sports Illustrated* Magazine wrote a three-part series titled "Sports and Religion." The writers covered many subjects, including the large sports ministries of Fellowship of Christian Athletes (FCA), AIA, and Pro Athletes Outreach (PAO), of which AIA was a part. While informational in nature, the tone of the articles carried some mocking criticism for the ministries' methods and strategies. There was very little mentioned of the thousands of people who were genuinely helped and encouraged by the athletes in these ministries. Even though they were called "jocks for Jesus" in the article, these athletes were providing meaningful answers and solutions for people trying to find purpose in the lives.

The legal challenge against public prayer and talking about Christ would sometimes hinder or even stop AIA's wrestling presentations. In October 1973, an attorney from California created a summary of the law for AIA regarding public prayer and openly sharing one's faith. In fact, he noted the First Amendment of the US Constitution specifically permits free exercise of religious speech and prohibits the government from stopping or mandating it to be a specific way. The US Supreme Court at that time heard cases concerning required Bible study, required prayer in a school, and religious activities "sponsored" by a government entity, and all were declared unconstitutional.

However, a school could legally accommodate a religious talk as part of the religious tradition of America. In 1970 the court affirmed this concept, and in 1972 the court said high schools could have invocations and benedictions at high school graduations. The attorney suggested it was acceptable under the law for a nongoverning authority to invite AIA to speak at presentations in public high schools. In other words, a coach, teacher, or school group could invite the team to speak. Or the school principal could make the assembly voluntary.

What about the school that wanted AIA to speak but had "political" resistance? Creativity was needed to provide the answer. For example, in Baton Rouge, Louisiana, the east team had a match scheduled with LSU (Louisiana State University). The CRU staff had several high schools that wanted the team to speak to their students, but a big assembly was a political "no-no." The AIA wrestlers and the school decided they could speak instead to every girl and boy's gym class—therefore reaching almost the entire student body. One challenge … the AIA group of three wrestlers had to present six forty-minute programs in a row! By the time the last gym class started, the wrestlers were an exhausted crew and almost giddy. With an audience of seventy-five to eighty girls in the gym class, two "pro wrestlers" (Skunk Man and Country Hicks) decided to run into the bleachers chasing each other and see what would happen. When they started the chase, the girls screamed bloody murder and starting jumping off the bleachers while others were falling over each other, stuck like turtles on their backs in the bleacher footboards. It took five minutes to restore order as the girls' coaches corralled them back into their seats. But at the end of the day, dozens of students committed their lives to Christ and had loads of fun with the wrestlers.

Another incident occurred in Boston. The high school wrestling coach loved AIA and wanted the team to do an assembly. The principal agreed, but one teacher protested before the assembly even started. Four wrestlers showed up for the program, but the principal told them they could do the assembly but could not pray or say God or Jesus. After some discussion, the men and the principal decided to do the assembly anyway. Instead of saying "God," the wrestlers simply substituted "my Father" or "your Father." When they would normally say Jesus Christ, they substituted "my Father's Son" or "your Father's Son." The assembly went on without a hitch! The wrestlers told the students how they tried to fill their empty lives through money, fame, and sports stardom but their lives were empty. They found their answer when they talked to "my Father" or "your Father" and surrendered to "the Son," who forgave them and changed their lives. Every student and teacher knew exactly what the wrestlers meant. The whole culture in the school was changed thanks to a coach's wish, along with some creativity from the wrestlers.

The year 1976 was pivotal as several of the AIA wrestlers had the potential to make the US Olympic team for the Montreal, Canada, Olympic Games. After the 1976 dual meet season, every athlete refocused on qualifying for the Olympic trials, hoping they would be peaking for this every-four-year extravaganza. Since AIA had won the team national AAU Freestyle Championship in 1975, the guys were ready to bring it on! The best wrestlers in America met in Cleveland to qualify for the final Olympic trials and a trip to the Olympic team camp. Nine AIA men qualified. Gene Davis and John Peterson made the final US freestyle team for the Montreal Olympics, where John garnered the gold medal and Gene won the bronze.

The average person does not understand or comprehend how difficult it is to make an Olympic team in any sport. It is extremely challenging and can be brutal emotionally and physically. For example, in the sport of wrestling in 1976, a wrestler first had to qualify by placing at a high level in one of several prequalifying tournaments. Then he had to place in the top three spots of his weight class in the national Olympic trials in Cleveland. If he placed in positions four, five, or six or was a special invitee because of injury or circumstance, he could compete again in a one-day mini-tournament at the final Olympic camp. After the mini-tournament there were only four men per weight class left. Starting with the fourth-ranked man, he would have to win the best of two out of three matches against the third-ranked man. Then they went up the ladder to the point where third challenged second and then second challenged first. It was a grueling and grinding journey! The body ached with wrenching pain and bruising. But through the rugged trials, one man wound up number one on the team in his weight class. He was then a member of the US team unless he got injured in training camp. Now he had the privilege to go face the top wrestler in his weight class from the other thirty competing countries, all trying to win the gold medal. If he failed to make the US team, he had to wait four long years to complete again. In reality, each athlete was indeed fortunate to get even one opportunity to make an Olympic team as a competitor for his or her country.

In international competition, each sport can be rife with politics behind the scenes. In the 1970s the Soviet Union controlled many countries through the communist networks. The communist countries were never really sponsors of "amateur" athletes anyway, since everyone worked for the state. Every athlete had been chosen as a gifted youngster and sent to a sports institute to be trained as a subject of the state, many times leaving his or her parents for months at a time. The coaches would become substitute parents. These "amateurs" worked countless hours every day every year, focused on their particular sport, and were paid by the government to train. In contrast, a successful American athlete made it happen with the help of parents, coaches, schools, and sometimes scholarship money ... quite a difference from a communist system.

Wrestling is the "hard work" sport, an endurance sport. There is no way to wrestle casually; it is simply too demanding on the body. For John and Gene, there was no shortcut or easy path to the pinnacle of the Olympic team. The AIA wrestlers did have "jobs" and worked tirelessly on the road traveling and speaking, rarely having a vacation or break. Vacation for most of them consisted of going home through August to mid-September each year to raise more financial support from their sponsors. Gene and John were coaches with AIA, plus competing wrestlers. As coaches, sometimes they had to get creative on the road to keep the athletes in shape and sharp enough to compete.

When not traveling, the AIA teams tried to work out twice a day. At 7:00 a.m. they would alternate running a few miles and lifting weights every other day and then practice on the mats each afternoon. When on the road they would have to improvise. In 1971 at a CRU college Christmas Conference in Dallas, the team was in a downtown high-rise hotel, with no gym or spa. So Coach Davis just had the guys run up and down the stairwell again and again—all fifteen floors! A wrestling mat never looked so good to the guys after that week of practice. Improvised soccer and basketball games dotted the practice schedule when a mat was not available, as well as running on roadsides and getting lost sometimes jogging in strange cities. "Basketball" games provided workouts for wrestlers sometimes. It was a lawless game where fouls were not called unless blood was drawn or an eye was poked. Everything else was legal. And they kept score!

As part of the US Olympic team, Gene and John journeyed to Montreal in June 1976. Several other AIA teammates traveled there too, including Larry Amundson, Henry Shaffer, Reid Lamphere, and a few others to participate in a small Olympic outreach ministry. Larry's wife, Ellen, was seven months pregnant, but her physician agreed she would be safe for the ten days that Larry was three thousand miles away in Montreal. They lived in Long Beach, California, with their three-year-old son, John Mark.

The AIA wrestlers who were unsuccessful at the Olympic trials returned home. Among them was Greg Hicks, who returned to AIA headquarters in Orange County, California. Greg's wife, Sue, was eight and a half months pregnant with their first child, so they would settle in to await the birth while enjoying the Olympics on television each night. One night just after the broadcast, Sue started labor pains, and Greg quickly took Sue to the nearby hospital. With Greg as her Lamaze coach, he helped Sue with breathing techniques and provided encouragement during the fifteen hours of labor, but eventually a C-section was finally performed. Little Cari Susette Hicks was brought into the world. Sue was assigned to stay in the hospital four days to recover from surgery and begin nurturing her newborn.

Exactly one night later, at 2:00 a.m., Greg received a call at home from Henry Shaffer, and the conversation went like this:

Henry: Greg, this is Henry. Did I wake you?

Greg: Of course you woke me. Why are you calling me at 2:00 a.m.?

Henry: Ellen Amundson is in labor!

Greg: But why are you calling me?

Henry: Larry is here with me in Montreal, getting dressed to catch a plane. Can you call Ellen and see if she is okay?

Greg: Sure, I'll do it right away.
        (Greg hung up and called Ellen, who lived twenty-five miles away.)

Greg: Ellen, this is Greg.

Ellen: Oh, hello Greg, Why are you calling?

Greg: I heard you are in labor!

Ellen: Who told you that?

Greg: Henry Shaffer.

Ellen: How did *he* know?

Greg: He's with Larry in Montreal. Are you okay?

Ellen: I called the doctor and he says I am having early birth pangs but to just come to his office in the morning. I am doing fine.

Greg: Okay, I'll pick you up at 7:00 a.m. and drive you to the doctor. See you in a few hours.

After Greg hung up, his adrenalin was rushing and he knew he would never go back to sleep. He thought of Ellen being alone with her little boy and Larry being three thousand miles away. He thought about Sue's struggle with the birth, so he called Ellen back.

Greg: Ellen, this is Greg again. I'm wide awake and you may be going into labor early. I'm coming now to be at your house in case you need me.

Ellen: Okay, come on. You can sleep in John Mark's bed.

At 3:30 a.m., Greg stumbled his way to John Mark's bed, and Ellen went to her room to endure the pains until 7:00 a.m. Greg woke up to the smell of bacon, eggs, and toast. Ellen, with labor pains twelve minutes apart, had cooked breakfast. What a trouper! They ate quickly and hit the freeway to the doctor's office, driving down toward Orange County.

While driving down the freeway, terror struck Greg's heart as he realized he was going to meet with the same doctor and see the same hospital staff that was caring for his wife Sue and their new baby! And he was walking back into the same reception area with another pregnant woman!

Ellen's contractions were even closer as he helped her into the doctor's office. A nurse quickly assisted her into the exam room. Greg found a corner chair in the lobby and hid his face as best he could behind a magazine. Within three minutes, the doctor walked into the reception room with Ellen by his side and in front of everybody announced what was going to happen next.

Doctor: So, Greg, are you going to be Ellen's coach today?
Greg: No, no! I'll be the assistant coach until Larry gets here from Montreal.
Doctor: Sorry, Greg. You're the head coach today. Larry will never make it in time!

Like a lightning bolt the thought hit Greg, *Oh my, how is Larry going to feel about this?*

Ellen and Greg drove off to the same hospital and walked to the same admissions desk toward the same nurses on the same hospital floor as Sue was staying. Their hearts were racing when Ellen said, "Oh, I forgot the camera!"

As a good coach, Greg said, "Oh, don't worry, not a problem. Sue is just down the hall and she has our camera!" Greg rushed to Sue's room but was stopped by a sign on the hospital suite door that said "Do Not Enter, Nursing Mothers."

In desperation, Greg yelled in a loud whisper through the partially closed door:

Greg: Hey, Sue!
Sue: Greg, is that you?
Greg: I need the camera!
Sue: What are you doing here?
Greg: I'm here with Ellen.
Sue: What is Ellen doing here?
Greg: She's in labor and she forgot her camera.
Sue: But what are you doing here?
Greg: I'll explain later. Just give me the camera.

Sue hobbled out of her bed and brought the camera to Greg as her three suitemates sat in stunned silence. Greg's heart was really pounding as he rushed back down the hall to Ellen's prep room. The doctor ordered Greg to put on his scrubs for delivery. Still unsure of this "coaching" decision, he went to Ellen, who was lying in her bed waiting to go into the delivery room. Greg asked her again if she was sure she wanted him to be her coach. She grabbed his hand and said yes. Greg looked over at the doctor, as if asking for advice, and the doctor just smiled.

It was on! Ellen was wheeled into delivery with Coach Greg faithfully following. Within an hour, little Linne was born—seven weeks premature!

Greg grabbed his camera when a nurse held Linne up for her first photo. "You must be a proud father," the nurse said with a wonderful smile on her face.

"Actually … I am not the father. My wife, Sue, is down the hall. We had our baby here two days ago," Greg replied sheepishly.

With that the nurse exclaimed, "Well … I *thought* you looked familiar!"

Greg got out of his scrubs as soon as possible. Exhausted, he went down to his car in the hospital parking lot, camera in hand, and slept until Larry arrived. After all, Greg had only one full-night's sleep in the last three days and had helped deliver two babies! Three hours later, Larry landed at LAX and drove like a madman to the hospital in Orange County.

A very nervous Greg walked into Ellen's room, and Larry gave him a big bear hug and thanked him profusely ... to Greg's great relief. Talk about teammates going beyond the call of duty! Being a *midwife* was tougher than wrestling a national champion!

Greg and Larry caught up on the details of the last few hours and had a good laugh. During a moment of quiet, Larry looked down at his feet and started laughing. In the chaos of dressing in the dark to catch his flight, he had put on one black shoe and one brown shoe. But it really did not matter. He was finally there with Ellen and a healthy Linne ... that was what mattered! Sue and Ellen became roommates for two days, while little Cari and little Linne became little AIA sisters for life with the same head coach.

> "A man of many friends comes to ruin, but there
> is a friend who sticks closer than a brother."
> (Proverbs 18:24)

Chapter 8
Touring Brothers for Life

God does not give us overcoming life. He
gives us life as we overcome.
—Oswald Chambers

1968–78

When traveling for weeks on end and living with host families in college towns across America, lifelong friendships are permanently forged. The engaging and difficult lifestyle of going into "combat" on the wrestling mat every day at practice or against another team and being on the point of the spear in spiritual warfare will make a person totally dependent on a teammate having his back. Even more important, you had to be totally dependent on God to accomplish anything significant spiritually.

This team was truly unique in every possible way, and a special team culture developed because they simply had no other choice. What other organization on earth would have the head coach of a team submitting to the leadership of the team director (who was a fellow wrestler) directing a staff-planning meeting, and an hour later go to wrestling practice and have the team director, in turn, submit to the coach's tough demands? The coach was in charge of practice … period. Remember, everyone was a wrestler first but had other key team duties as well. What organization would have a new rookie staff member/wrestler being personally trained in every skill imaginable by a senior AIA staff member/teammate, and an hour later the new staff person could kick the senior staff member's butt on the wrestling mat at practice?

Everybody served everybody and submitted to the authority above him when appropriate. It takes a special breed of brother to function in this way, alternatively submitting to the leadership of a brother or leading a brother, depending on the circumstance in which they found themselves. If an athlete could not get over this "love your brother, serve your brother, lead your brother" culture, he did not stay around too long.

Team prayer was also a big part of the team culture, and the teammates prayed together about everything—traveling safety, athletic injuries, speaking engagements, financial support, family issues, and personal problems. They had to be vulnerable and open about personal problems. They prayed constantly for God to lead them in everything they did and to use them always to influence others for Jesus Christ. Prayer was their lifestyle, personally and together. Memories are etched deeply and seared forever into the brain inside a team environment such as theirs. After a decade of US and worldwide traveling in the trenches, both in and out of the glare of the public spotlight, these men and women were permanently changed for the better. Their true experiences were both serious and funny, with some being so amazing they almost seemed made up. They are not!

The Single Guys

The single guys started their unique lifestyle and traditions in the old mountain cabin in 1968 in the San Bernardino Mountains of Southern California. That first year set the stage. When the team moved from Southern California to Oklahoma City in 1969, the single guys split up into apartments for the first year but decided to consolidate again into one house in September 1970 to save money and share cars. They chose a small, old, framed white house in a neighborhood in Edmond, about ten miles north of Oklahoma City. It was a quaint fifty-year-old wooden house with dirt for a yard, which was just what they needed—no maintenance required! The yard only had a few blades of grass, which allowed lots of room for parking cars. With their travel schedule, the last thing they wanted was a manicured yard and a beautiful home to care for. It was the perfect bachelor pad because they could not mess it up too much, plus the rent was cheap.

New AIA teammates joined Larry Amundson as the senior staff member, who became the "den mother." They included Gary Rushing from Arizona and Nick Carollo from Adams State (one year veterans) plus rookie Brian Dameier from LSU. They had so much to learn as rookies and things got interesting from the beginning.

Brian reported to the team really short of cash. As he drove up from New Orleans, he discovered that his small paycheck from CRU got messed up in the mail. He prayed mightily on the long drive for God to solve the cash problem as his hunger grew stronger by the hour. He begged God to provide for his needs. God quickly answered his prayers. New teammates Kent and Maryanne Kershner drove into town that day from Montana with their car loaded with fresh meat from the "hunt." (Montana men and women love to go hunting and fishing, so they had ice chests full of elk, moose, and deer meat.) Kent had no freezer to store such a haul of meat, so he gave a bunch away to his new AIA teammates. Brian volunteered to take pounds and pounds of the protein-rich meat off Kent's hands. Just like the complaining children of Israel in the wilderness in the Old Testament, God gave them doves until they almost vomited from eating bird meat. Brian came close to doing the same thing in Edmond as God answered his prayer.

Larry and Nick had gone with Gene Davis and Greg Hicks the summer of 1971 to the US World Championship team trials at the Naval Academy in Annapolis, Maryland. After the rugged tournament tryouts, Gene made the US team at 136.5 pounds, while Greg was awarded an alternate team position at 180.5 pounds. Greg and Gene would stay at the Academy for three weeks of training camp before heading off to Bulgaria. Larry and Nick did not fare as well and decided to hop in Larry's car and drive straight through to Edmond, Oklahoma, a mere one thousand miles away. Sue Hicks and Frances Davis, Greg and Gene's wives, decided to stay at camp a few days longer and then go slow and easy back to Oklahoma.

Larry and Nick drove long and hard straight through. It was hot and sticky weather, but they drank lots of coffee and finally got home about two o'clock in the morning. They opened the door to the hot stuffy house and quickly turned on the air conditioner to cool things down. It had been weeks since anyone had been there, and they stumbled over things trying to remember where everything was. Being so dreadfully sleepy, they just crashed. Larry mentioned to Nick that the place smelled bad, but fatigue took over and they quickly fell asleep. At midmorning they finally woke up to a bright sun and got up to make some coffee. Larry showered and noticed again that the smell was really bad and he told Nick that they needed to check the place out. After looking around for ten minutes, they found the answer. Unfortunately, a small animal was lying dead as a doornail directly under Larry's bed! After yelling at each other to "clear the air," they quickly provided a small funeral for the poor creature.

When the team divided into east and west teams in the fall of 1972, the single guy's tradition continued to live on. The east team single guys set up an apartment at first to live together but later rented a farmhouse in their new home base of Lancaster, Pennsylvania. Senior team leader Reid Lamphere was in charge of the group. John Peterson, recent Olympic silver medalist, joined the team, along with newcomers Eddie Rew of Auburn University, Mike Pratt of New Mexico State, heavyweight Mike McCready of Northern Iowa, Mike Whitfield of Buffalo, and Kyang Mu Chang, a South Korean National Champion and Olympic team member.

Mu Chang was called "Mu" by his teammates. Mu was a most unique AIA team member, being a star athlete in Korea who spoke little English. Like his AIA predecessor in 1968, Mitsuo Nakai from Japan, Mu came to America to share the love of Christ with Americans. Even though he knew little about American culture, he was really outgoing and eager to learn. It was going to be on-the-job training for Mu in the language and culture. Mu's adventures started very quickly in Lancaster. He loved to eat, and even though he was a small, stocky 134-pounder, he could eat as much as the heavier athletes. The single guys loved to eat out rather than cook, so they would regularly go out to the all-you-can-eat restaurants, especially the pizza places. He and John Peterson would each eat an eighteen-inch pizza at one sitting!

Mu was once invited to eat with some teammates at wrestler John Hart's parents' house for a home-cooked meal. Mrs. Hart was a great cook, and she served a dozen ears of freshly picked corn. Mu ate seven ears very quickly, along with the other food.

Mrs. Hart said to Mu, "You must really like corn on the cob."

Mu replied, "I no eat, I die!" He had learned English pretty well, particularly when it came to food.

Another time Mu went into a convenience store and brought out a frozen can of Welch's grape juice concentrate and a spoon. He tore the top off and began to eat. Sue Hicks tried to explain that he needed to add lots of water to create a gallon of grape juice. Mu looked up and smiled and just kept right on eating like it was ice cream!

Eddie Rew recalls the fun times with Mu at the single guys' place: "I was excited about my flight up to Lancaster and joining AIA to be a part of a team that used wrestling to share their faith in Christ. I flew out of Atlanta, one of the largest airports in the United States, and landed in Lancaster, Pennsylvania, one of the smallest airports in the United States. There to meet me was new teammate, Bob Kuhn. Bob, who was married to Lynn, told me he was taking me to the single guys' apartment. I was looking forward to meeting all the guys, but to my surprise there was only one person there—Kyung Mu Chang. The problem was, Mu could hardly speak English, and for a guy from Alabama, that was a big problem. Most of our communication was by hand gestures and friendly grunts.

Mu was preparing a rice dish with hamburger. It was enough to feed about ten people. So when he motioned me to eat, I had no problem joining him in trying to eat a gallon-sized pan of rice and meat. My first introduction to Mu and AIA was a sign of things to come.

"One day Mu asked if I would take him to the local mall called Park City, touted as 'big enough to be a city; nice enough to be a park.' We could use teammate Dave Pratt's car. I had some shopping to do and off we went. When we got there, Mu wanted me to park at the far end of the parking lot where there were no cars. It was a strange request, but I was beginning to realize that was to be normal for Mu. I went in to shop, but he wanted to stay in the car and wanted me to leave the keys. I assumed he wanted to listen to the radio. *Strange,* I thought. I finished my shopping, and as I walked out of the mall I saw the car at a distance, jerking through the parking lot. Mu's plan was to use this time to practice his driving skills on Dave Pratt's manual transmission. Every time he put his foot on the accelerator, the car would lunge forward. Every time he tried to shift, he would hit the brake, throwing him against the steering wheel. As I watched Mu lunging his way through the parking lot—bouncing from seat to steering wheel—I didn't know if I should be angry for being tricked or just laugh at the sight of this funny guy learning to drive."

Eddie continues describing living with the single guys: "One night the AIA single guys decided to go out to a local attraction. The Green Dragon was a strange name for a place where townsfolk and Amish in Lancaster would go to buy leather goods, baked goods, vegetables, and crafts. It was a county-fair atmosphere without the rides or games. The most interesting part of the Green Dragon was the animal auctions. During the morning and afternoon, the larger animals were auctioned but at night the smaller animals were center stage in a scene right out of the movies. As you walked into the barn, wooden bleaches surrounded the stage where the auctioneer was about to electrify the audience of bidders. Straw covered the floor, and well-placed lights accented the fibers of straw that escaped the floor and floated through the barn as if they were an active participant in the drama that was unfolding. A man carried a box to the auctioneer and unveiled a small bunny. The excitement began. 'Who will give me a dollar for this fine rabbit?' One after another the bids came in. Chickens, ducks, guinea pigs, doves—you name it—and there was a bidding war. The thrill of bidding flooded over everyone there. Before long the single guys were raising our hands to bid—just for the fun of it. But we were champion wrestlers; we were trained to win. It was in our DNA. That night we brought four hens, four roosters, and two rabbits back to our new home—the farm the single guys rented. These animals would nicely replace the piranha that used to be in our living room aquarium in the apartment, as well as our bathtub that we stocked with goldfish for feeding our piranha.

"We were now real farmers with livestock. At least we thought. We didn't know a thing about animals, so we gave them their freedom. They could roam the acreage as they wished, eating whatever they could. After all, it saved us from buying food and feeding them. We quickly learned that roosters not only crowed at dawn (when self-respecting wrestlers are asleep), but about anytime they want, day or night. Roosters also like to protect their territory—especially from small human beings. This created a problem because part of our rental agreement was to allow the landlord's daughter to use the house for daycare one day a week. Attacking chickens was not part of the deal. It was time to do what farmers do … eat our free-range birds. We made a deal with John Peterson, the only real farmer on the team, to pluck and prepare half the chickens.

"The big day arrived and John came prepared. He brought all he needed to get the job done. It was our job to catch the birds. There were four of us. John and I plus wrestlers Mark Dymond and Dave Mulnix were the chicken-plucking team. The problem was, Mark and Dave were recovering from knee surgery and moved around on crutches. They agreed to whack the chickens with their crutches when the chickens came near them. Let the games begin! Chickens, like most creatures, don't like being caught and killed. Chickens can be quick. I don't think I ever laughed as much, seeing the four of us chasing after those chickens. Once they were caught John made quick work of the preparation. All we had to do was cook and eat our prey. Dave Hannah, the director of Athletes in Action was visiting us in a couple of days, so John decided to host our leader from California one of our free-range birds for dinner. We put the rest of them in the freezer until someone could tell us how to cook chickens. Anxious to know how the meal went with our boss, we found John the next day and asked. He said, 'Those were the toughest chickens I have ever eaten.' We left our frozen fowl in the freezer and never bothered to eat them. I think they were still in the freezer when I left the team a couple years later."

On the Road

The teammates were traveling for weeks on end for thousands of miles in any kind of vehicle they had. Minivans or station wagons were the luxury transportation vehicle if available. The vehicles were packed to the limit with suitcases, duffle bags filled with workout gear, Christian materials for events, and toys for little kids, if needed. Shoulder to shoulder for miles and miles, for hours on end, the travel eventually became uncomfortable. The travel stories are legendary, as told in their own words.

Eddie Rew

It was a joy to travel with our teammates and spouses, but after days and weeks of traveling together you looked forward to the time you got away by yourself. On a return trip we started talking about how we were looking forward to our alone time. Each of us had a plan that didn't involve anyone else on the team. As each person proudly shared his plans for the days alone, you could see the worn faces of a long trip light up with the anticipation of time away from the team. I shared my plans to see a movie that I had seen years ago, one of the funniest movies I had ever seen. The day came and I drove to the theater without having to wait on anyone. I was all by myself, with just me to please. As I stumbled down the aisle of the darkened theater I noticed teammate Dick Pollock and his wife, Julie. I couldn't believe they were here to watch my movie! So I automatically started to sit down next to them. As my eyes became adjusted to the darkness I saw the seats next to Dick and Julie were filled with the other members of the team! They had all come to my theater. There we were all together, even when we could have been in a dozen different places. I got to the last seat on the row and sat with the rest of the team and watched the movie. I guess that's what families do.

John Klein

On the first ever tour trip to Oklahoma, we spent one night on the road and two grueling days driving. We were so short of money that the single guys got a motel room meant for three and slept six in the room. We made it work by taking mattresses off the beds and hide-a-bed and laid them on the floor, while the other guys slept on the box springs. And it was a Motel 6 to boot, for only $19.99 a room per night! In 1969 we were traveling through the Big Sky country area of Montana toward Colorado. Montana had no speed limit on the major highways so we were flying about ninety mph. Our car suddenly got stopped by a highway patrolman, who was suspicious why so many people were stuffed in a car with an out of state license plate. When we told him we were with the AIA wrestling team trying to get to the University of Colorado, he asked if one of our teammates had a Chevy Camaro with a racing stripe. "Yes, that would be Larry," I said. The patrolman said, "I thought so, because he was flying down the road a hundred miles an hour a little bit ago!" The cop let us go on to Boulder.

Henry Shaffer

On one of our long trips the married men, wives, and kids sometimes traveled together. We had our son, Solomon, with us, along with Gary and Maryanne Wallman and their little boy. Their little one had a smooth, round, bald head, so the team nicknamed him "Nikita" for Soviet leader Nikita Khrushchev. For traveling with kids, we rigged our van up with a platform to cover from the back seat to the very back of the van. We stuffed the bags and gear under the flat board and laid a blanket on top so the kids could sleep and lay around for our hours on the road. We stopped to get gas and all of us went inside the station for a potty break. We then realized Nikita was missing. We ran back out to the van and it was empty. In a panic we rapidly looked everywhere around the building, but Nikita was nowhere to be found. Suddenly I looked behind the platform and saw the shiny top of a little bald head. Nikita had slid down and was wedged straight up between the van back door and the platform. He never cried but was content to be wedged in there stuck like a bug!

Dan Moskowitz

The team was in Columbus, Ohio, for a match with Ohio State, and we were making the usual rounds at area high schools doing the standard AIA assembly presentation. One of the programs scheduled was at the Ohio State University student union building. When we got there they had set up a stage with a spectator area and the place was packed with between one thousand and fifteen hundred students. Reid Lamphere, Rick Greene, and Mike Whitfield were with me. The program proceeded smoothly and we are really connecting with the college students, just like we did in high schools.

We got to the part where we demonstrate the neck strength of a wrestler by doing an arching back neck bridge, where one wrester lies on his back and arches his chest up with only his head and two feet on the mat. We did it with a person standing on his chest ... always an audience favorite. As usual, Reid looked around the room and called for the biggest person in the room to step forward to help us demonstrate. Suddenly the crowd started chanting. At first I could not make out what they we chanting but then we clearly heard,

"*Hugee, Hugee, Hugee*" over and over. I didn't realize the significance of this until I saw a student from the back of the crowd start moving forward. Reid and I must have spotted the student at the same time, because we both turned to look at each other, and I will never forget the look on his face. It was a combination of shock and amusement.

This student was every bit of four hundred pounds, and maybe more. At that time this was easily the biggest person I had ever seen in person! My mind went to work thinking, *I can't do this. He's too big. How do I bow out in front of all these people? I will embarrass the team. I am going to* die*!* But for the team, I had to go through with it. Reid had called out for the biggest person, and this guy would qualify in any crowd that wasn't made up of pro football players and circus freaks.

Without any clear sense of how to bow out without shame, I proceeded to get into a back bridge position, arched my back, and prepared for the worst. Normally one of the wrestlers will help the individual onto the bridging wrestler's chest so as not to create sudden excessive pressure from the step up. As "Hugee" approached, I saw one of the other wrestlers step forward to help Reid in assisting this individual as he stepped onto my chest. I closed my eyes and felt him place his foot on me and step up. I could tell he was being supported by my teammates, and then suddenly I could tell he wasn't. I remember feeling the hard floor against my head through the mat, and everything started to go black. Even with my eyes closed it seemed like everything was getting darker. And then he was gone, or I thought, *Maybe I am gone to be with the Lord!* I suspect this was the shortest duration for any neck bridge in AIA history because once they helped Hugee up, they released him for a second and then helped him off. I don't know whether it was to save the reputation for AIA or save my life, and frankly I didn't care. I successfully had maintained the bridge and still had feeling in all my lower extremities. The crowd went wild! I guess they had suspected I would collapse immediately and when I didn't, that was good enough for them. I will say that was the last neck bridge I ever did with AIA and I had a stiff neck for the next fifteen years.

Greg and Sue Hicks

We were in Macomb, Illinois, to wrestle a Saturday night match against Western Illinois. The CRU staff hosted us for about five days that week prior to the big match, and they packed the schedule with at least thirty different speaking engagements for the team. We were busy speaking mornings and into the late evenings. Our host family was the head football coach's family who lived in a nice neighborhood in a nice new development. The houses all had a similar look to them, and there were not too many trees along the streets. We were so busy our hosts told us to just come and go as we pleased … just act like we were one of the family!

On the third day, Sue and I were picked up by different people to do speaking engagements with different teammates in different places around the city. At about eleven thirty in the morning, I came back and was dropped in front of our host house. By then I had forgotten the exact address, but usually the coach's wife's brown car sat out front. So I just got out where the brown car sat and walked in to the split-level house. I went down the stairs to the closet and was taking off my coat when I turned to see a frightened woman with her hands to her face.

"*Who* are you?" she shouted.

I said, "I am Greg. And who are you?"

She answered, "I live here, and you are in my house!"

Shocked, I explained who I was and that my guest host was the football coach.

She relaxed a bit and said, "Oh, they live next door, and you are in the wrong house."

After a good laugh, I apologized profusely and walked next door.

About fifteen minutes later Sue got back from her engagement and walked in the coach's house, laughing out loud. She said, "Greg, you won't believe what just happened. I walked into the wrong house, and this lady walked up and asked who I was. I told her I was Sue Hicks and she said to me, "Do you have a tall red-headed husband?"

Bob Anderson

John Hansen and I were at a small college in Missouri. We had a meeting set up to speak to a fraternity, and we were eating dinner with them before we spoke. They were laughing and talking about how drunk they were last night. One of the guys had shot his dresser drawer full of holes with a pistol, putting bullet holes in all his underwear. They were holding his underwear up and laughing about how crazy he was. After dinner we were introduced as the AIA wrestlers for the match that week and began to speak about Christ. John Hansen and I gave our testimony, but the reaction was not that good at first. Some of them invited us into the living room to talk more about what we had said. After a few minutes of discussion, I asked a couple of guys if they would like to receive Christ and they said yes! So I asked them to get down on their knees in front of everybody and ask Christ into their hearts. They did!

Then one of the guys ran up to his bedroom and came back down holding a Bible. He said, "My mother said I would need this." We dusted it off, and they began to ask questions for a long time. After that exciting time we walked out the front door and couldn't believe what God had just done.

As we were leaving, John said, "Do you hear that?" He heard music and was so excited he thought maybe God was trying to say something to him.

I said, "John, that's dance music."

He said, "Jesus went to the temple, so we're going to the dance."

So we walked into the dance hoping to talk to some college kids about Christ, but there were hundreds of kids dancing to the loud music.

John said, "God will show us." Just then the music stopped and about six kids sat down in the middle of the dance floor.

John said, "I guess that's who we're supposed to talk to."

We went over, started talking to them, and got into a debate about God. As John was debating, two of them started talking to me. After a few minutes of answering questions, both of them prayed to receive Christ right there on the dance floor in front of everybody.

John Klein

In 1970–71, during the fall and spring months when the team was not touring, we worked with college students at Central State University in Edmond, Oklahoma, just north of Oklahoma City. In the student union one day, Bob Anderson and I were meeting with the only Christian football player we knew, a guy named Phil Thompson. Phil pointed over to the far corner of the cafeteria and told us a bunch of football players were over there eating together.

So Bob asked, "Who is the grossest guy on your team?"

Phil pointed toward a big defensive lineman.

Without saying a word, Bob stood up, waltzed up to the big lineman's table, and asked to talk with him. Within minutes, Bob had whipped out the little "Four Spiritual Laws" booklet that the team used to share their faith. Bob challenged the football player to become a Christian. A few minutes later, Phil and I looked over in awe from across the cafeteria seeing the player bow his head and praying to receive Christ.

Later that month at a football game, the player invited Bob to meet his parents, so Bob shared Christ with them too. Phil Thompson later joined the CRU full-time staff after graduating.

Tom Keeley

We wrestled the New York Athletic Club in 1975 in a dual meet on Long Island, New York. The NYAC and AIA had become big rivals at the National Freestyle Championships with their teams fighting for the national championship trophy for several years. A club team dual meet with teams going head to head was very unusual. But what a challenge it was. A large crowd of almost two thousand people packed the gym. The match was a battle royale, and the score was close going into the heavyweight match. Carl Dambman had just joined the team and was not yet physically fit to wrestle. He was up against a former Syracuse wrestler who was an NCAA runner-up.

Carl had to pin him in order for us to win the match. But it looked like that would never happen as Carl was getting thrashed 9–0 with only a minute to go, and both wrestlers were so tired they could hardly stand up. His opponent shot in for a double-leg takedown to end the match with a superior victory and secure the win for the NYAC. Carl sort of turned his hip a little and grabbed his opponent's head and shoulder for a headlock, taking the guy to his back. With time running out, the referee raised his hand to signify the fall and we won the match! As sportscaster Al Michaels said in 1980 when the US team beat the Russians in hockey, "Do you believe in miracles?" Our team bench exploded, and it was one of the greatest athletic experiences I have ever been part of.

After an hour of celebrating, we were getting into one of the team cars to drive back to Lancaster, Pennsylvania, because we had to get up early the next morning for a two-week tour of the Midwest. Somebody had accidentally locked the keys in one of the cars. So we had to scramble to find accommodations for that night and get the local car dealer to bring a master key the next morning to get in and finally get on the road, a half a day late.

"All things will work together for the good of those who love God and are called according to His purpose" (Romans 8:28).

Later that spring at University of Indiana, the east and west AIA teams combined to compete at the national AAU freestyle tournament. Our big rivals again were the NYAC, and they were there in full force with all their studs from all over the country, former national champions and all-Americans. The team title was closely contested up to the final few matches of the championship. Mu Chang was wrestling his final tournament match to determine third place in his weight class. If he won, then that clinched the team championship for AIA; if he lost, then NYAC would take the first-place trophy. Mu pulled out a close match and we were crowned the national AAU champions, making us the best amateur wrestling team in the United States, dethroning the NYAC, who had won the title many times previously.

Eddie Rew

We were scheduled to do an assembly program in Richmond, Virginia, at a local high school. The people who invited us were excited about the assembly and much burdened for the hearts of the students at the school, so the teacher in charge of the cheerleaders started a twenty-four-hour prayer chain for our visit. We arrived early in the day only to find out that the assembly would have to be *after*, not during school. We were told by many people there that no one would stay after school. The school gym would be virtually empty. Over and over again we heard the same story, "'No one stays after school," so not to expect many at the assembly. Carl Dambman, our heavyweight wrestler, was also Baron Von Crusher, his character in the pro-wrestling skit. He decided he would dress up in his costume and make some noise that afternoon during school hours.

Carl quickly found a "promoter" in the form of the school janitor who joined Carl in the cafeteria and the gym classes to hype the upcoming wrestling program. The closing bell for school finally sounded, and students began pouring into the gym. The bleachers were totally full. Students and teachers canceled meetings and doctors' appointments to hear four crazy guys give a wrestling demonstration and talk about Jesus.

The team asked the janitor to be part of the assembly program as the wrestling promoter. He played the part perfectly. He walked in with Carl by his side and shouted out to the students, "What makes this man so big? Was it spinach?"

The students yelled, "*No!*"

"What makes this man so strong?" The janitor reached in a box and held up a bag of doughnuts.

The crowd shouted, "Doughnuts!"

Again he yelled, "What makes this man so powerful?"

"Doughnuts!" they shouted.

The students responded amazingly, and it was all because a few people chose to believe God and committed themselves to prayer, plus a janitor who loved the Lord and pro wrestling!

Frances Davis—Brothers and Sisters Get Together

Sue Hicks and I were with our husbands in August 1971 at the Naval Academy, living temporarily in our pickup truck camper. Gene and Greg lived in the dorms with the US team while working out twice a day. When they left for the World Championships in Bulgaria, we left for home in Oklahoma City along with my toddler, Mark. Going from Annapolis to Oklahoma City was a long, hard drive. Along the way we noticed a big fourteen-wheeler pull up beside us, but he wouldn't pass us. Finally we looked over to see him pointing to our tires and motioning us to stop. We nervously pulled over.

He got out of his truck and showed us that our left rear tire was almost flat and we were in the middle of nowhere. He proceeded to change our tire and put on the spare. We thanked him profusely and shared our faith with him. He was already a Christian, and as we drove off we thanked God for His mercy by allowing a brother in Christ to come to our rescue.

Sam Hieronymus

My new wife, Jan, and I were traveling with Tom Talbert and some AIA guys to speak at an all-night youth rally in Turlock, California. It was at a high school gym and we gave an evangelistic talk at 1:00 a.m. Jan was so sleepy by then; she slid down to rest between the bleachers. As other teammates left after I spoke, I looked around the gym to find my wife, but she was nowhere to be found. So I assumed she left with some of the other AIA guys. I went back to our host house, only to find Jan was not there! I panicked and raced back in my car toward the gym. My heart sank as halfway back I found my wife walking aimlessly down the road under a streetlight, just crying her heart out. Not a good way to start a marriage. I assured her the AIA wrestling lifestyle was an exciting one. And thankfully she forgave me!

Sue Hicks

In 1971 we were driving back to Oklahoma City after leaving the team to finish a part of their tour in the Southeast. I drove our car and my AIA passengers were team secretary Faith Bode and wrestlers Mitsuo Nakai and Colin Hudson. It was a nine hundred-mile drive but we decided that we could make it in one shot since there were four drivers. Our little Pontiac Tempest was loaded down and the trunk was full of bags and materials from the tour. Late that night, Mitsuo was driving and the rest of us were sleeping. Suddenly we were startled as the car bounced and jerked right, which jarred us awake. Mitsuo kept right on going and calmly said, "Sidewalk." Apparently he had dozed off.

Colin freaked out and demanded Mitsuo let him drive. Mitsuo refused. So when we came to the next small town and came to a stoplight, Colin jumped out of the passenger side, ran around to the driver side, and banged on the window. Mitsuo did not budge and sat there until the light turned green and started to move forward. Faith and I yelled to stop, and then all four of us were yelling at each other. To get things settled, I told everyone that it was my car and I was driving all the way back to Oklahoma. So I took over. Then at about three o'clock in the morning we were driving through the middle of downtown Memphis, Tennessee. Suddenly I saw a flashing light behind me. I stopped and waited for the policeman to walk up. He flashed his light on all of us and asked us what we were doing there at three. Then he made me get out and open the trunk. He looked in it and asked who we were and where we lived. We explained about the AIA team and we were heading back to Oklahoma.

He laughed and said, "The reason I stopped you was that your car was so low down in the back I suspected you to be bootleggers trying to get though Memphis in the middle of the night." With AIA, we had been accused of being a lot of things, but never bootleggers!

Dan Warren

The pro-wrestling skits were the funniest things I remember, with Don Zellmer as the Baby Hulk all decked in green muscles and Tom Talbert as Captain America. I was Darth Vader, so Rich Hay got a Darth Vader costume and helmet from a contact in Hollywood. When I was introduced at the first part of the skit, my opponent would walk up and give me a sharp bop on top of my head, and the helmet would split apart into two pieces! Our announcer would then say, "Wow, it looks like Darth has a splitting headache!" Actually, the helmet had to come apart in two pieces so I could complete the wrestling skit with a black ski mask on. Mike Whitfield was my other favorite pro-wrestler opponent, as he would come out riding his stick-horse onto the mat, wearing his big oversized cowboy hat. He was "Buffalo Chip" from the Wild West.

★

Over the years, the tens of thousands of miles of traveling by the teams were a highlight and sometimes a grind. There was never a dull moment on the road. They ran over deer and punctured gas tanks, lost keys, and sustained injuries skiing in zero-degree winters and while playing touch football barefoot on the beach in the summer. They sometimes talked cops out of speeding tickets and stayed in guest homes a few times where they felt sequestered to their room with little food. They also met wonderful and friendly people all over America who truly loved the Lord and who were a great blessing and encouragement to them. They met people who bought meals for them, housed them for free, let them borrow cars, and gave them free tickets to local events. It was all part of the Master's plan. And He was not finished yet!

"Commit your works to the Lord, and
your plans will be established."
(Proverbs 16:3)

East team wrestler Brian Dameier speaking
at a college match during halftime.

Pregame prayer in the locker room before a big match.

Team speaking at a college wrestling match.

National Federation Freestyle Team Champions, 1971.
L to R standing: Gene Davis, Bob Anderson, John
Lightner, Greg Hicks, Henry Shaffer, Nick Carollo,
Larry Amundson, John Klein. Seated: Gary Rushing,
John Hansen, Gary Wallman, Doug Smith, John Hart.

Legend Dan Gable takes top position against
AIA wrestler Gene Davis at the Southern Open,
1970. In 1972, Dan won the gold medal and
Gene the bronze in the Munich Olympics.

Travel woes on the team tour ... Sue Hicks sits on top of a gas pump in the snow in Wyoming.

A lightweight wrestler demonstrates amazing neck strength with the largest man in the gym standing on his chest during a high school assembly.

East team wrestler Reid Lamphere juggles
oranges in a classroom as the teacher
and children look on with delight.

An AIA wrestler speaks about his faith in Christ
at a high school assembly in the school gym.

The AIA west team, 1973. L to R: John Weber,
Kent Kershner, Pete Noble, Jim Axtell, Tom Talbert,
John Lightner, Nick Carollo, Larry Amundson,
Mark Dymond, Phil Paladay, Doug Smith, and Gene Davis.

Wrestler Greg Hicks speaks to a large
group of college students on campus.

Chapter 9

International Explosion

A Christian worker is one who perpetually looks into
the face of God and then goes forth to talk to people.
—Oswald Chambers

New World Coming
1977–78

When the east and west teams started their season in 1976, they were well received on college and high school campuses. Everywhere they traveled and spoke the people responded to the wrestlers' message and strong athletic performances. During the midseventies, the two AIA wrestling teams combined were regularly speaking to well over one hundred thousand people per year, primarily students.

The teams were winning about 90 percent of their matches against college squads and were much respected in the wrestling world. Like it or not, winning covered a multitude of sins … meaning that since Christianity suffered from an inferiority complex, it needed a positive makeover in the public arena. Most people thought Christianity was for weak people or people who desperately needed a crutch to prop up their feeble self-esteem to make it through life. The wrestlers were physically tough, successful athletes who crushed the myth of weak Christians and gave new meaning to the term "men of God." Often they would do unique things to prove the point. In January 1978, west team heavyweight Bob Walker, after a little encouragement from his teammates, decided to challenge a brown bear on the wrestling mat! Yes, a huge brown bear named Victor, standing more than seven feet tall and weighing 562 pounds, was part of the entertainment package for the Sports, Vacation, and Recreation Vehicle Show at the Anaheim Convention Center. The big bear had won more than two thousand wrestling matches against all takers before he met Bob. The *Orange County Register* sent a reporter and photographer to document the momentous match. Sure enough, the 245-pound heavyweight AIA wrestler handed Victor his first loss. The newspaper the next morning showed a picture of Bob with hands raised high, squatting on top of the big bear. Victor had no comment after the defeat!

Over and over the men on the team received amazing comments from their presentations. At a college match in Virginia, students responded on comment cards after a dual meet:

"When you talked about trusting God in a relationship of love, not fear, I thought that may be the answer to my relationship with Him. Do please send me more information!"

"I thought you said it very well. I give my life to Christ."

"I let Him into my life. Because of you, God is now my best friend!"

The teams were getting incredible access to different groups of students at the universities in more than just athletic teams, dorms, fraternities, and sororities. At Central Michigan University, the local CRU college staff asked professors if the team members could bring a Bible-based lesson to their classes if it was relevant to the professors' curriculum. So the wrestlers and wives received invitations to create talks related to physical education, home economics and even a philosophy class.

It worked remarkably well as the wrestlers and wives fanned out into the selected academic classes, reaching students on the intellectual level, not just the athletic or social levels. In one philosophy class Greg Hicks taught about "The Truth Found in the Bible" in three consecutive morning classes. After two rather awkward introductions by the professor in his first two classes, by the third introduction he said to his class, "Listen to him carefully because it is true!" Maybe the third time was the charm.

Over the years the team began to have two parallel sets of goals: using sports to reach out to college and high school students, teachers, coaches, and fans; and penetrating the international sports community by qualifying athletes for international teams and traveling worldwide. With more spiritually mature athletes and more world-class wrestlers on the teams, both goals could be achieved. Since a few of the original AIA team members had rotated off the team into "retirement" over the years, newly recruited wrestlers were filling every weight class and keeping the team competitive and complete.

In 1977, team director Larry Amundson approached the US wrestling governing body, the AAU, to ask if an AIA team could represent the United States in a world-class international tournament. The AIA basketball team had already completed similar trips to a couple of countries. The AAU officials surprisingly said yes, so the planning for a big international tour began in earnest.

The tournament chosen was the now-defunct Aryamehr Cup, hosted by the Shah of Iran in Tehran. It was one of the premier wrestling tournaments in the world, with top powers such as Russia, Bulgaria, Japan, and other countries competing. Wrestling is the most popular sport in Iran, and Iran always has one or more world champions on its teams. AIA jumped at this chance to represent the United States!

The AIA team was well represented with two Olympians, Gene Davis and John Peterson, plus others with international experience including Reid Lamphere, NCAA champion Steve Barrett from Oklahoma State, Sambo wrestling heavyweight Carl Dambman, and new AIA all-American wrestler from Arizona State, Don Shuler.

The team also tacked on a trip to Bulgaria, a country that loved sports but was under the firm grip of the Soviet Union. Wrestling and soccer were the national sport obsessions there. The purpose of visiting Communist Bulgaria would be strategic since the spiritual outreach was going to be more one on one with coaches, sports administrators, and athletes. The idea was to make contacts with top sports officials while competing against the best athletes and presenting the message of Christ one person at a time. It was a carbon copy of the original method the AIA wrestling team used years earlier when competing in dual meets against the United States' top college wrestling programs. "Taking the team to Bulgaria" was the original dream of Pat Matrisciana and Dave Hannah, and it was finally coming true ten years later. The only thing the team could not do in Bulgaria was speak to large groups of people.

As the 1977 trip to Iran and Bulgaria was so successful, with several wrestlers placing in their weight classes at the tournament, and for making future key contacts, the AAU and AIA agreed to go back to Iran to compete in the Aryamehr Cup again in 1978. This time they tacked on a trip to Poland after the tournament. Because of these successful trips, Bud Hinkson, the CRU European director, began to ask the AIA wrestlers if they would come to Europe to headquarter there. He knew without sports that he would never meet key people in communist countries and the AIA wrestlers could provide the means to reach his goal.

The 1978 trip to Iran came under extremely different circumstances. The Shah was under heavy attack by Islamic revolutionaries in Tehran. The timing of the international wrestling tournament was unfortunately in the middle of the internal political upheaval.

AIA wrestler Mike McArthur described the events that occurred from his perspective: "Mark Johnson from Michigan and the future world champion Dave Schultz traveled with us on the second Iranian Tour in 1978. After a few days of preparing for the tournament, the Russian team continued to spy on us as we worked on technique in our morning workouts. Coach Davis decided we'd run up the mountain behind our facility for a morning workout. The whole team set out very early that third day, and our goal was to reach the top of a fairly significant mountain. Four of us—Don Zellmer, Gene

Davis, Dave Schultz, and I—eventually reached the summit. As we looked at the massive expanse of mountain ranges to the north, we also noticed far below a convoy of military vehicles on the backside of the mountain. They looked minuscule, but we could see them unloading the trucks and beginning to shoot their rifles into the mountainside. We figured it was simply firearms practice, but the dirt that was thrown up from their bullets was getting closer and closer. Dave and I were standing about fifteen feet apart when a bullet zipped between us. I wouldn't have known what the sound was, but Dave, being a gun buff, knew exactly what it was—a bullet. Realizing they were shooting at us, we looked at each other and realized we both had 'USA' printed on the front of our warm-ups. We were obvious targets, to say the least!

"We quickly began our descent down the backside of the mountain to the facility. That's when we found out that terrorists had sprayed warnings on the buildings and the tournament had been canceled. We were advised to leave the country immediately. When arriving at the airport with our interpreter, he had us stay on the bus while he went in to find out our next move. Upon returning to the bus, he directed the driver to leave the airport and drive to his apartment in Tehran. God had obviously done a work in his heart as he hid seventeen of us in his apartment for three days and two nights, with his wife and two children staying there also.

"Don Zellmer and the interpreter went to the market to get dates and other food items that kept some food in our bellies for those few uncomfortable days. Our bathroom facilities at the sports complex were simply a hole in the floor and two foot pads. But at the apartment they actually had toilets. In fact, they had two in the one bathroom. One was up on a pedestal and that's the one Don Zellmer decided to use. But it wasn't a toilet, it was a bidet. He found that out when he flushed and got a shot of cold water … a little humor in a tense situation!

"We somehow got on an airplane that others were not able to board, and off we flew to Istanbul, Turkey. We did have an emergency stop in Beirut, Lebanon, where the first person to board the plane stepped on the lady's foot who been moved up front to lie on the floor after convulsing. That sent her back into convulsions. They carried her off the plane, and we had armed military personnel standing guard around the perimeter of the plane. After a couple of uncomfortable hours of simply waiting, they closed the doors and off we went. Only God knows what happened to the poor woman who never reentered the plane!

"They served some type of quiche on the plane, and Mark Johnson got so sick he couldn't walk or talk for some time. We carried him to the airport medical facility there in Istanbul and finally prayed over him as we relented to letting a crusty-looking doctor give him a shot from a very unsanitary medicine bottle and a steamed needle. We found a lady who interpreted for us and she assured us this muscle relaxant would help him. It finally did, and he said to me when he could finally talk a full day later that if he ever got that sick again, he knew the Lord was taking him home!

"When we reached Poland through the intervention of prayer and some political maneuvering, more interesting events took place. We all visited the second-largest concentration camp from World War II. It was certainly an eye-opening experience and showed the depravity of mankind at one of its lowest points. We witnessed among other things a man with a Gulf Oil baseball cap on, weeping, standing in front of a wall-length picture of three male prisoners in the camp. Every picture in the place could certainly bring a person to tears, but for some reason this one seemed different. Most of the inmates were executed in that camp. A few days later, as we were preparing to fly home from Poland, we saw this same man with the baseball cap who we'd seen at the concentration camp. Jody Sloan and I went over to him as he also recognized us. We asked him why that one picture affected him so much. He explained in broken English that he was a little boy when his father was captured and put into that camp. His dad never returned home, and one of the men in that picture was his dad. Wow! We were able to talk a bit with him about our team and our mission. We prayed with and for him as we parted."

Team director Larry Amundson remembers the story from his leadership position: "While we slept one night, terrorists broke into the compound and spray painted onto the walls of the buildings and buses: 'If this wrestling competition continues, athletes will die.' The Iranian wrestling federation immediately canceled the tournament and told us to go to our embassy. This was the same embassy that would be occupied for more than a year while Jimmy Carter was president. Our embassy was not much help. They said the situation was tense, but they didn't know of any imminent danger. They suggested we leave. We had flown in on Pan American Airlines, and they wanted hundreds of dollars to change the tickets for our flight to Poland. Plus, our visas would not be valid for several more days in Poland. I assure you I had no problem praying as I felt the weight of responsibility for this team of almost twenty people and for their safety. I was calling my wife, Ellen, in the United States, having her call the AAU leaders in Indianapolis to see if we could go into Poland early without a visa. Each day I would go to Pan Am, Iran Air, and other airlines to see if we could leave without this huge charge to change our tickets. Finally we were allowed to leave with no charge as long as we did not change our routing. We were leaving on Iraqi Air. When we got to Istanbul, our flight to Warsaw was canceled, and we were put in a nice hotel and rescheduled on Austrian Air into Warsaw the next day. The Polish Wrestling Federation met us, and we entered the country with no problems.

"Here is what I learned from those first two trips abroad: God used the wrestling team to help us open up our AIA international ministry. We had a model for future trips on how to visit hostile places. On those two trips we could see the guys that were cut out for international ministry. I always say when you take twenty people overseas on a tour, about fifteen can't wait to get home. On those trips, Reid Lamphere, Carl Dambman, Don Zellmer, Steve Barrett, and John Peterson all stood out. I remember on that first trip to Iran how John Peterson looked out over the city of Tehran and said, 'I could get excited if God called me here.' God used the team to open up CRU ministry in Bulgaria as well. Bud Hinkson was our official team leader when he traveled with us. The wrestling team was to become the model for AIA sending summer teams internationally in all sports."

Mike remembers the irony of the trip. "Just a few months later, seventeen US hostages were taken in Tehran's US Embassy and held for 444 days. We had met two who eventually became hostages. One was a friendly guard from the US Embassy, and a teacher, Dr. Keogh, from Illinois, who taught at the American school there in Tehran. We were able to do our famous AIA assembly presentation during our first couple of days in Iran at the school."

Some people might ask why God would allow these men, who are sent out to serve Him, to land in Iran and sit there doing nothing for days in a dangerous situation. Why would they have to suffer this way, worrying about their personal safety and the lives of their wives and kids thousands of miles away? Oswald Chambers gives some insight: "Sorrow removes a great deal of a person's shallowness, but it does not always make that person better. Suffering either gives me to myself or it destroys me. You cannot find or receive yourself through success; you lose your head over pride. You cannot receive yourself through the monotony of your daily life, because you give in to complaining. The only way to find yourself is in the fires of sorrow. If you will receive yourself in the fires of sorrow, God will make you nourishment for other people."

Something big was being stirred inside the individual hearts of that team by God Himself. From the team that traveled to Iran in 1978, the five AIA wrestlers that Larry noted would be in Europe working full time within the year, leaving the United States behind. Larry would become the international director of all international sports, team tours, and tournaments. Soon other teammates would follow these pioneers. Instead of discouraging the wrestlers who were concerned for their safety in Iran while under severe political pressure, the trip actually lit a fire in them!

These men in their mid- to late twenties, most married, were willing to leave the comforts of the United States, sell all their possessions, and move to a land not even knowing the native language. What would possess these men to do this? Mere logic does not provide a satisfying answer.

What is the possible answer? The apostle Paul explores the answer as he was compelled to drop his career path and his advanced education to travel in danger all over the Middle East and southern Europe in the first century. He writes to the Corinthian Church, "For the love of Christ controls (constrains) us … we walk by faith, not by sight (appearances) … also, we have our ambition to be pleasing to Him … therefore, we are ambassadors for Christ!" (II Corinthians 5:7-20). The love of Christ is a most powerful force! His love drives people to be "ambassadors" representing His kingdom, regardless of the danger or risk.

Oswald Chambers writes, "Paul says he is overruled, overmastered, held as in a vice by the love of Christ. Very few of us know what it means to be held in a grip of the love of God; we are held by the constraint of our experience only … Paul says he is gripped by the love; that is the only reason he acts as he does. Men may call him mad or sober, but he does not care; there is only one thing he is living for, that is to persuade men of the judgment seat of God, and the love of Christ."

So these wrestling men of God packed their bags for Europe after the second harrowing Iranian trip. Europe would become their home not for a one- or two-week stint but for much of their adult lives. Even to this day those foreign lands are still "home" for a few of them.

What makes the men of AIA so tough, so resilient, and so persistent? What creates the never-surrender, never-give-up attitude? Why are they so driven to "fight the good fight"?

First consider that wrestling is combat—man against man! It is not only the world's oldest sport and one of the most demanding sports, it may well be the world's toughest sport. Conditioning for the sport is grueling and must be constant, not sporadic. Most guys who try out for the sport quit after just a few weeks of painful workouts, never to return. The personal commitment to be a successful or just an average wrestler separates the men from the boys. Discipline and self-motivation are paramount.

Cutting weight and starving to make weight at weigh-ins takes as much effort every day as competition in the match. For some AIA wrestlers, there were days of skipping meals and hours of sitting in a hot sauna wearing rubber suits to sweat off the pounds … after a full wrestling practice! No body fat or excess body fluid was the goal, and sometimes even standing up too quickly would make a wrestler feel faint! After staggering on to the scale to make weight at official weigh-ins, they would run to grab a drink of liquid and scarf down oranges and honey for strength. In tournaments, they had to weigh in every morning for several days. That meant jogging in rubber suits or sitting in the sauna late at night after wrestling in matches, or before dawn before weigh-ins. As legendary wrestler and coach Dan Gable said, "Once you've wrestled, everything else in life is easy!"

Secondly, wrestling is not for the athlete who craves great public glory and fame. He spends endless hours in small, cramped, hot wrestling rooms, with sweaty mats covering the floor and spreading halfway up the walls. Wrestling fans do not see the hours of practice and personal sacrifice it takes to simply have the privilege of competing head to head for six to twelve minutes on the mat. There is nowhere to hide once the competition begins on the mat. Only one man wins, every time. The other man leaves as the loser, every time. And then the routine starts all over the next day for the next match, with another grappler who wants to take your head off and crush you into the mat! It takes great personal courage and nerves of steel to step out onto that mat.

But the AIA wrestlers experienced much more than personal athletic acclaim or fulfillment. They chose to follow Jesus Christ and to follow Him fully! When people fully abandon all to Jesus Christ and feel the pull of God's hand on them, they will become a force for the cause of Christ. They will not easily cave into pressure, or avoid hardship and difficult circumstances. This step of high commitment is a pivotal singular personal decision in life, followed by a lengthy process of working through real-life circumstances. "You willfully place yourself in the Potter's hands" (Jeremiah 18:4–6).

AIA founder Dave Hannah often said, "God never said it would be easy." The writer of Hebrews says, "The Son of God learned obedience through suffering" (Hebrews 5:8). Each AIA wrestler and each wife went through the tough personal decision to believe and trust in Christ … for everything. This decision to join the AIA team came with the challenge to leave careers, home, family, and personal goals … to travel constantly, share their faith with strangers, speak to groups publicly, and raise their own financial support! And asking people for money to support the ministry, in itself, is incredibly humbling and imposing. You must cast your ego aside and raise funds for the greater cause. To join the AIA team full time, all these things became mandatory. The process of deeper commitment is both fascinating and lengthy, without a predesigned formula. It is a life of abandonment and dogged faith! It often brings the sting of being misunderstood by others. The results, however, are extreme fulfillment and personal joy! They became ambassadors for the cause of wrestling and, more important, for the cause of Christ. Ten years and counting—where would it lead them next?

> "If you are slack in a day of distress,
> your strength is limited."
> (Proverbs 24:10)

Chapter 10

A Divided Europe

When we are certain of the way God is going to work, He will never work that way again.
—Oswald Chambers

The Second Decade Begins
1978–83

God works in mysterious ways. He uses every human decision for a purpose, both good and bad. In 1978 the AIA national leaders decided due to the changing landscape in the world of sports and the financial costs of traveling teams that it would be wise to consolidate the east and west wrestling teams to one new athletic facility in Fountain Valley, California. The new facility would house a wrestling workout room, a gymnastic school facility, and the national headquarters office for all Athletes in Action members.

For the wrestling team members, this created a difficult decision, particularly for the east team located in Lancaster, Pennsylvania. The west team families were located in Long Beach, California, and would not have to move. They would only need to drive every day to a new practice facility in Orange County—twenty miles away. But the east team would have to pack up everything and travel three thousand miles west to relocate. The prospect of moving made everyone reevaluate their future.

Meanwhile, CRU European director Bud Hinkson had been hoping the east team would not relocate three thousand miles west, but three thousand miles east—to Europe! Maybe this was Bud's opportunity to bring the wrestlers there to help with the growing European ministry, particularly in Communist Eastern Europe.

After some prayer and a little encouragement from Bud, four wrestlers and their families decided to move to Vienna, Austria, to start a new east team headquartered there.

A few of the team members decided to leave the team and return to their chosen careers, and several other teammates moved west to join the west team. With the west team now fortified with more wrestlers, they would continue to dominate athletically on the mats and effectively minister for several more years on the college campuses in America. The European team would forge a new sports outreach using wrestling competition and speaking opportunities similar to the American strategies.

The original wrestling team had evolved over the first ten years. Some of the wrestlers and their wives now had children, while many of the single men had married and were starting families. Team rosters changed every year as new men arrived and a few men moved off the traveling team to pursue other opportunities.

The new recruits who joined AIA's national championship team had interesting requirements to be invited to join the team. Ironically, they did not have to be an all-American, win the NCAA tournament, or even win their conference championship. All they had to be was a decent college wrestler. Imagine a national champion freestyle team not requiring new athletes to be superior at their sport or at the top of the pedigree! Not so for AIA. They required foremost a heart for God, a teachable spirit, a strong desire to improve athletically, and a good work ethic. That was it. Yet they improved athletically dramatically over the years. Athletic super-talent was not the primary requirement, although several NCAA all-Americans joined the team.

The team expected each athlete and wife to develop their personal God-given talents, regardless of what they were, all for the glory of

God. So fittingly, John Hart, who was not the highest-powered athlete, played the guitar and led singing at various meetings. Dave Pratt, not a conference champion, used his talent of juggling with tennis balls and apples to bring joy to thousands of students in the high school assemblies and college campus meetings. Brian Dameier, not an all-American, used his speaking talent and humor to train dozens of AIA athletes in the techniques of communication and public speaking. Jim Schmidtke was not even a wrestler when he joined the east team as the advance man. He traveled ahead of the team's arrival on campus and set up dozens of meetings to maximize the team's impact while on a campus. He promoted the world-class Polish Greco-Roman national team coming to Lancaster, Pennsylvania, to battle with the freestyle wrestlers in a sold-out Franklin and Marshall College gym. The AIA star freestyle wrestlers had never wrestled Greco-Roman style, but they "sacrificed their bodies" in a different style of wrestling in order to share their faith. US world team members Greg Hicks, John Peterson, and Mike McCready all got pinned in matches against the world championship silver medalist Greco team, but no matter! Jim went on to become the AIA national and international leader in ministering to athletes and coaches in soccer, the world's most popular sport. On the AIA team, each person would blossom as God used each member's various talents and gifts for Him.

Sometimes new recruits would join the AIA team for one or two years and then leave the team to pursue other opportunities. Several left to become wrestling coaches and teachers in middle schools or high schools. Steve Gaydosh became the most successful high school wrestling coach in Alabama history. Many became college coaches: Steve Suder (Wyoming); Neil Turner (Lock Haven University, PA); Gary Clark (Taylor University in Philadelphia); Don Shuler (Liberty University); Dan Hicks (Cal State Fullerton); Jesse Castro (Liberty University); Mike McCready (Upper Iowa). Rich Pollock coached at Waynesburg College, went to seminary to become a pastor, and then later coached high school. Tom Keeley and John Weber left to attend Dallas Seminary. Some left for other ministries: Doug and Jackie Rickard—*The Jesus Film*; Art and Sue Holden—Wycliffe Bible translators; John and Carol Weber—chaplain for the NFL pro-football Dallas Cowboys; Bill and Kay Gifford—Fellowship of Christian Athletes; Tom and Linda Talbert—CRU in the United Kingdom. John Hart became a professor at Moody Bible Institute. Gary Rushing coached at Minnesota State. He as well as Dan Sherman are currently college professors. Some started new ministries after leaving AIA, such as Henry and Linda Shaffer, who started a ministry called Won by One to Jamaica, and Mike McArthur started a ministry called Fellowship of Christian Cowboys for the professional rodeo circuit. Mark Dymond became an elementary school principal, Eddie Rew an elementary school athletic director. These and many more wrestlers used the AIA training and experience to propel them to careers and meaningful lives.

This is not to imply that all the AIA athletes and wives were free of problems or never faced serious trials and tribulations. They were normal people in every way and dealt with the same issues that all people face. Being in the public eye and being involved in spiritual warfare as members of such a unique team brought stress and scrutiny.

The teammates were there for each other regardless of what difficulties arose. Each and every struggle was handled in the appropriate way for the overall team goals and each individual's best interest as a cherished team member.

The four east team wrestlers and their families who relocated to start the European team were fulfilling part of AIA's original worldwide vision. When the decision was made to combine teams in California, circumstances began to be orchestrated by a sovereign God that the national AIA leadership had not originally planned. The small group packed up for Europe and in particular for Vienna, Austria, which became the headquarters in 1978. The national AIA leadership team soon embraced the shakeup in their long term plans.

The initial challenge was immense. First there was the language barrier. This small group of pioneers went full speed into German language school five days a week, three hours a day for ten weeks on and ten weeks off. Several years later two team members moved to Moscow, when the Iron Curtain fell, and began the hard work to learn the Russian language. These efforts to learn the native tongue would be rewarded a hundredfold as the years went by.

Second, Europe in the late 1970s was a split continent as a remnant of World War II when Lenin and Stalin took control of Eastern Europe and ran it with an iron fist, using Communism and the Marxist philosophy to govern. Traveling behind the Iron Curtain was a major issue, but sports officials, coaches, and athletes did not have near the difficulty that normal civilians from the west would have.

The third issue was the secularization of Western Europe. A strong Christian community was not to be found in free Europe. The Reformation of Martin Luther happened hundreds of years earlier. The flowering and spread of Protestantism had died out. The Enlightenment, which was based on the philosophy that humans would be able to solve all known problems, had taken severe setbacks with two world wars in Europe by the mid-twentieth century. Hitler and Stalin had crushed the Enlightenment philosophy that man was basically good. Man's inhumanity to mankind had been on full display in Europe, whether it was the blood-filled trenches and mustard-gassed bodies in World War I, the Holocaust of Adolph Hitler against the Jews, or the Gulag of Joseph Stalin.

Churches in Europe were either relics of historical architectural beauty in Western Europe or converted to warehouses and storage places in Communist Eastern Europe. The first permanent wave of AIA wrestlers and their wives enthusiastically embraced this split culture. They were ready to create something out of nothing, by the grace of God—just like the original AIA wrestlers had done a decade earlier in the United States.

Reid and Carolyn Lamphere and Reid's cousin, Tom Lamphere, Carl and Noreen Dambman, and Doug and Barb Klenovich with their two children took on an entire continent. They would create the outreach and ministries as they went—totally by faith—that God could lead the way and open new doors. And they would compete and train in the sport they loved. Fortunately for them, in many communist countries, wrestling was a very popular sport.

Within a year or so the 1980 Olympics in Russia were boycotted by the United States and other countries over the invasion of Afghanistan. After only two years, three new US-based AIA wrestlers, John and Nancy Peterson, Steve and Cindi Barrett, and Don and Robin Shuler joined the team in Vienna. Steve and Don were NCAA All-Americans, and all three wrestlers had extensive international wrestling backgrounds. Having Olympic champion John Peterson on the team would open even more doors.

The AIA group realized that wrestling was *not* the only sport Europeans loved, so they started to bring US college all-stars from other sports such as soccer and basketball, particularly to Eastern Europe behind the Iron Curtain. The wrestlers and other athletes were able to share their faith carefully and quietly within the communist borders. The response was quite positive because of the respect and quality of the US athletes and the team leaders. Spiritual seeds were being planted over and over, regardless of politics.

The world of sports is valuable in so many ways. One of the greatest benefits is that sports can quickly break down language, cultural, and political barriers. Almost everyone loves sports in general, and most people are sports fans to some degree. Athletes are famous and popular but are real people, so the average person wants to meet and know them. Someone once said, "An hour of sports is like a year of conversation." Reid discovered that almost no one in Europe could believe an athlete could also have a college degree. That alone was a conversation starter. But no one in Europe had ever met a top athlete who was a college graduate and also a Christian. Now that was a novelty and a curiosity worth talking about to the Europeans!

Carl Dambman remembers a key trip in 1981. "The AIA team took a trip to a wrestling training facility in Poland to work out with the Polish national team. After a six-hour drive we arrived at midnight. Immediately thereafter, the Soviet Army declared martial law and shut down the border. The Soviets did not like the freedom movement called Solidarity, which the Polish nation relished. The USSR leaders decided the heavy-handed approach was the only solution to quash the movement.

"At the Sports Hotel over the public address system an announcement was made to inform guests and hotel staff that in twenty-four hours, all foreigners and domestic citizens were required to have military permission to travel. The Polish people were in shock, and the announcement brought great fear. All the police and army athletic clubs, including wrestlers, had to report for duty. There were massive public protests in every city in Poland. The AIA wrestlers went into prayer to ask for God's guidance—should they stay or leave? Would they risk arrest or jail? No one knew.

"The wrestlers were up in the mountains with no means of communicating with their families back in Vienna. The guys decided that God had sent them there and they were staying! On Monday, they asked the Polish coach if they could share their purpose and speak with the Polish team after practice—just as they had done in the United States with college teams. After dinner, all the wrestlers and coaches met in a room and the AIA guys shared a couple of personal testimonies of their relationship with Christ through an interpreter. The Polish athletes asked question after question. After two hours, one AIA wrestler suggested, "Let's take a break." The Polish wrestlers said almost in unison, "*No*, hear more!" For two more hours the AIA wrestlers talked with thirty Polish wrestlers and coaches about God, Christ, and the Bible. It turned out this was just the beginning!

"At the request of the Polish athletes, the AIA team continued the spiritual training for four additional nights, with two hours of Bible study each evening after wrestling practice. In this stressful climate of military takeover by the Soviet Army, the Polish athletes were ready and hungry to hear about hope and spiritual freedom. How ironic that only seven years earlier the Polish Greco wrestling team had journeyed to Lancaster, Pennsylvania, to wrestle two of these AIA wrestlers, Reid Lamphere and John Peterson. Polish Bibles were given to all the Polish athletes, and now John and Reid were on Polish soil teaching out of the same Bible.

"At week's end the AIA team received permission from the army to leave Poland. At the border, the army searched their bags, which were minus a few Bibles and some Christian literature. The army allowed them to leave quietly. The Polish wrestlers and coaches had all the Bibles! Had the military declared martial law one day earlier, none of this would have happened. God's invisible hand is real!

"Many times after that amazing week, the AIA men were invited back to practice wrestling and provide spiritual training with the Polish teams. Soon the up-and-coming younger Polish wrestlers were invited to the training camps. Each night AIA wrestlers would mentor and speak to the wrestlers about God and Jesus Christ, teaching the truths of the Scriptures after the afternoon wrestling practice sessions."

On a trip in 1983, the AIA wrestlers stopped at the Polish border for a baggage check. The border guards found packets of Amway's Nutralite Vitamins and assumed they were drugs. Actually the vitamins were intended to be gifts for the Polish wrestlers. The guards reacted when a sniffing dog got excited over a gift bag. After holding the AIA wrestlers for eight hours while a lab tested the vitamins for drugs, the sniffing dog then fell in love with an old pair of smelly wrestling shoes in Carl Dambman's bag. After some laughs and apologies the guards sent the team on their way.

Some countries were held in a tighter grip than others by the communist governments. Romania, Bulgaria, and Yugoslavia were tougher to access. This limited the AIA team in some ways. Poland and Hungary were easier places to make headway. It was a patience game of building relationships over long periods of time. These relationships would pay off handily in just a few short years. Because of the sensitive nature of the Eastern European strategy, things had to be somewhat of a secret.

John Peterson remembers how it was early on: "Don Schuler and I were traveling through Italy to get to Nice, France. That trip happened because of a lack of clear communication between Reid and me. We were at a tournament in Hungary shortly after my arrival in Vienna. While at that tournament, Reid told me, 'Do everything you can to schedule a competition in France!' I thought that was a crazy idea since we had moved to Europe to work to get the gospel into the countries behind the Iron Curtain. However, being the 'always submissive' staff member that I was, when the French delegation asked me if we would come to their tournament in Nice, I said, 'Sure, we will be there!'

"Back in Vienna, my excitement of having accomplished one of my first assignments from Reid was quickly squelched. I was informed that he did not literally mean France, he meant Russia! The CRU office used code names for the different countries we were working in for security reasons. Poland was England, Czechoslovakia was Belgium, and the Soviet Union was France. God still used the trip to France for His good. Romans 8:28 is true! We did end up building some relationships with the Bulgarian wrestlers while at the tournament in Nice. We even shared the gospel with one of our interpreters at the post-competition banquet."

After being in Vienna for a few years, there were too many security leaks, and with spying on the increase, the team decided to move its headquarters to a small suburb of Munich, Germany. The wrestlers found a good situation with a top German wrestling club and good workout facilities. Munich was near to the heart of AIA since the first Olympic outreach in 1972.

Exciting things continued to happen. In 1983, the wrestlers had a goal to get forty-four pounds of fresh bananas to the US team at the world championships in Kiev, in the Soviet Union. The AIA team drove from their Austrian headquarters. At the border checkpoint, the border guards confiscated the bananas because no fresh fruit was allowed to cross. As they searched all their bags, Carl Dambman and John Peterson would sneak a few bananas back into the bags they had already searched. The guards told them they would have to either eat the bananas or leave them. Wrestlers love competition, so they had a banana-eating contest! According to heavyweight Carl, he and Olympic champ John wolfed down eight bananas each while the others ate three bananas each. The guards were so impressed they let the team take a few of the remaining bananas with them.

Of course the guards searched their bags for any literature. Fortunately, Reid and a couple other wrestlers had memorized their gospel presentation in Russian, anticipating the guards would do a thorough search. As soon as they arrived in Kiev, they wrote down the presentation from memory, in Russian, so they would not forget it. They used the written presentation to share their faith whenever they had the opportunity to speak with athletes and coaches at the tournament.

Exchanging gifts and trading is a tradition at international sports events. Sports fans and athletes alike adore souvenirs such as lapel pins and flags, banners, or posters—anything that indicates they were attending or competing in a particular event. At the World Championships, a Russian coach came up to Carl and asked for a trade. According to Carl, the coach wanted to trade a Russian wrestling training book for a *Playboy* Magazine—illegal contraband in the Soviet Union.

Carl said, "I don't have a *Playboy,* but I have a book about God!" (Bibles were also illegal in Russia.)

The Russian was surprised but listened as Carl explained how a person can know God personally. The Russian coach gave his life to Christ! He told Carl he prayed with him because years earlier he had been held in prison and had overheard a minister talking about God to one of the prisoners. He never forgot what the minister said. "Now today, I am ready to pray," he said. Carl gave the coach the Russian Bible in exchange for the Russian wrestling training book before leaving the World Games tournament.

East Germany was one of the countries in which it was particularly difficult for the AIA guys to develop relationships. Perhaps the East Germans had something to hide. The East German athletes were long suspected of using performance-enhancing drugs, particularly their national women's swim team and their track and field athletes. No one could actually prove this since their government scientists developed ways to keep the drugs undetected. Except for East Germany, the AIA team over the next seven years was able to create good relationships with coaches, athletes, and government officials in most Eastern European countries.

One particular good relationship was with Czechoslovakia (currently two countries called the Czech Republic and Slovakia). AIA was able to bring Czech wrestling teams to their home base in Munich. The young athletes and coaches from the communist country jumped at the chance to go to free and prosperous West Germany for a visit. Wrestling workouts were just something they tolerated for the sake of visiting and touring around Munich. The AIA wives became heroines in the outreach to the Czechs. Part of the deal was the three AIA families would provide housing and food for the athletes and coaches at their own expense. The women would take four to six guys each and put them on couches or in sleeping bags all over their small houses. In addition, they would cook huge, tasty meals, which took hours to prepare for all these hungry wrestlers and coaches.

The wrestlers' wives routinely made huge sacrifices. Mind you, each wife was a mother to several children while they were hosting the Czech athletes in their home. Also just imagine seeing their husbands take off for days at a time into countries that were dangerous or hostile to Christianity. They were truly women of God, willing to serve Him and total strangers for the cause of Christ while raising their children and being supportive wives.

Relationships continued to be forged on the mats and in their homes. The Czechs became friends with the wrestlers and their wives. The AIA families continued to live out their faith in Christ with the visitors. Later the Czechs told them that it was how the AIA families behaved in their homes that impressed them most.

The team also presented dozens of wrestling programs to youth and Christian groups all over Western Europe in addition to the underground church groups behind the Iron Curtain. Doug Klenovich and John Peterson biked through the Austrian Alps, going from village to village holding wrestling exhibitions for the missionaries with Youth with a Mission (YWAM). They also did high school assemblies in Ireland with a Finnish Olympic medalist in track and field. Eastern or Western Europe, it did not matter to them, they went wherever an opportunity was presented.

Some trips were life changing and had long-term results. One such involved John and Nancy Peterson's relationship with a Romanian couple. John describes the amazing story: "My first trip to Romania was with Stephen Barrett and Don Shuler to a wrestling tournament in the mountain city of Brasov just north of Bucharest. It's a beautiful area tucked into the Carpathian Mountains. While there I met Jon Botceu, a Greco-Roman world champion who had been at several of our training camps in the United States during the late 1970s. Jon had come to many of the Bible studies that we had at those camps. His English was excellent, so we used him as our interpreter for much of the tournament. Sometime during that tournament Jon introduced me to his coach, Peter Stroe. Jon told me, 'Don't waste your time talking to Peter about Jesus; he is married to wrestling!' Peter knew some German, so I began a relationship with him that has carried on through the years. After Stephen and Don moved back to the United States for the 1984 Olympic trials and Reid and Carl moved to Munich, Nancy and I remained in Klosterneuburg, Austria. There were five of us CRU staff guys who were on loan to the Biblical Education by Extension ministry. They took over the old CRU office in Vienna. I worked as a facilitator and coordinator of the different groups of students in Romania. On each trip to Bucharest I would spend a night or two with Peter and his wife, Maria.

"For the first couple of years, Peter showed little if any interest in spiritual things. We talked a lot about wrestling and some about the evils of communism. Peter had been 'blacklisted' as a teenager for protesting against the system at the boarding school he was forced to attend. He spent one year in jail as a result, in a small room with a number of others never seeing the light of day! Because he was blacklisted, he was never allowed to compete outside of the Eastern Bloc countries. He had defeated the 1968 Olympic champion but was not allowed to be on the Romanian Olympic team. You can imagine that he had a lot of bitterness to deal with.

"From the very start, Maria showed interest in the Bible. Many nights we would sit together in their small apartment after an evening meal talking through questions she would ask. She would use German and Romanian Bibles as I used German and English ones. Peter would just sit by quietly. Gradually it became apparent that God was softening his heart and giving him a desire to know the Lord. He gave his life to Christ. I would often have one of our sons travel with me. Peter and Maria became like grandparents to our kids. They had relatives in West Germany, so in the summers when they visited them, they would stay with us on their way to and from West Germany. Then we moved back to the United States. Beginning in 1991, Peter came to the states each summer to work with Stephen Burak at our summer AIA camps and to work with my brother, Ben, and me at Camp of Champs. Through the years, God has used Peter to influence many wrestlers through the change that Jesus made in his heart!"

Powerful spiritual things were happening in Europe, whether visible or invisible, as the wrestlers methodically penetrated the veil of secularism in Western Europe and the communism of Eastern Europe.

"Like apples of gold in settings of silver is a
word spoken in right circumstances."
(Proverbs 25:11)

**Olympic bronze medalist Gene Davis
wrestles internationally.**

Gene Davis waves to the crowd in
Munich on the medal stand.

AIA wrestler Don Shuler wrestles in Europe for AIA.

At the World Championships in Istanbul, Turkey,
Gene Davis carries the flag for the US team as Greg
Hicks and Mike McCready follow in line, 1973.

**John Peterson prepares to receive the Olympic
gold medal at the Montreal Olympics, 1976.**

AIA heavyweight Mike McCready goes
head to head with four hundred-pound
Olympic bronze medalist Chris Taylor.

Chapter 11

Summer Camps and Summer Tours

Only a child gets prayer answered; a wise man does not.
—Oswald Chambers

1980–Today

Another amazing new sports ministry outreach started as a result of several AIA wrestlers in the United States who "retired" from the mat and headed to different locations. In 1980, AIA national leaders decided to send full-time representatives to the new National Olympic Training Center in Colorado Springs, Colorado. The first two couples assigned were Tom and Linda Talbert, members of the AIA west team, and Doug and Barb Klenovich, who moved back to the United States from the Europe team. Both Tom and Doug had wrestled in college against the AIA team while attending the University of Maryland and Clarion State, respectively.

The Olympic Training Center was a perfect spot for the former AIA wrestlers. Only elite US male and female athletes trained there in various Olympic sports, for the excellent coaching and the high altitude workouts. In addition, athletes from foreign countries in many sports visited the center to train, offering the AIA staff the opportunity to meet international athletes and coaches.

AIA decided to develop new exciting summer tours sending collegiate all-star teams to foreign countries for ten- to twenty-day trips. Essentially, the strategy was an expansion of the original 1967 AIA team tour to Japan and to some degree the 1977 and 1978 tours to Iran, Bulgaria, and Poland. The teams would be recruited and facilitated by the staff in Colorado Springs. These summer trips were win-win situations for everyone involved.

The AIA trained college athletes could share their faith in Christ all over the world with tens of thousands of people, many of whom had never heard the message of the Good News. Secondly, the tours provided a very strong spiritual, educational and cultural experience for the college athletes. There was daily Bible study along with training in how to share their faith with others in groups and one-on-one settings. Of course there was first-class coaching, training, and competition for the collegians. What an opportunity for college kids!

The impact was powerful and life changing for the collegians. Tom and Linda started recruiting teams to send to Central and South America. Meanwhile, Doug and Barb focused on recruiting and sending teams from various sports to Europe and Asia. Year by year the tours grew to the point that some thirty to forty teams of collegiate athletes were traveling to dozens of countries around the world each summer. The teams duplicated a tried and true strategy of competing in tournaments and against club teams or even national teams. While they competed in each town and village throughout the world, they spoke in churches, schools, prisons and at universities, always giving each person a chance to respond to them through interpreters.

Sometimes a trip would have a profound lasting effect on the college athletes on tour. One young woman who was a successful basketball player took an AIA trip to South America. She had become a believer in Christ when an AIA staff member spoke to her college team. When she was challenged to go on a summer tour, she jumped at the opportunity! Life was never to be the same for her after the trip. As she explained, "I never realized God could use my athletic talent for Him." Her love of her sport later led her into college coaching but she "was searching for answers inside." Full of questions and in frustration about her future, she cried out in prayer, "God, I'm tired of trying to figure this out. Just send me wherever you want and I will go!" A few weeks later after a phone call from abroad, she found herself on a flight to a foreign country. She had faithfully asked God to lead her to work anywhere with athletes and coaches and she quickly got her answer.

Since that time she has "multiplied" herself a hundredfold by following Christ fully and using her athletic and teaching talents. She also exercised tremendous courage despite all the odds against her. Some of her friends and family thought she was wasting her life and career. This reaction is similar to the Bible description of the disciples complaining about the woman who sat at Jesus' feet, *wasting* expensive perfume by wiping His feet. Jesus did not see it that way. He said, "She has done a good thing and wherever the gospel is preached, she will be remembered" (Mark 14:3–9). A sold-out life of service for Him is not a "wasted life" but a life valued by Him! She continues her work to this day.

Sometimes God does not provide spectacular results but instead provides "little miracles" that only He could achieve, just to remind us that all is well. Doug Klenovich tells an amazing story of one summer team in Europe comprised of both AIA wrestlers and college all-stars. "In 1982, Barb and I moved to Colorado Springs from Vienna, Austria. My first goal was to recruit a summer project wrestling team to Eastern Europe. God put together a great team that included Jim and Bill Scheer, Dave Schultz, Dan Cuestas, Clar Anderson, Randy Willingham, Karl Lynes, Tom Riley, Gene Davis, John Peterson, and others, plus six wives. The last week of the trip we were at the Czech/Poland border crossing into Poland. We were in two vans sitting on a bridge over a river between the two countries. The border guards took all our passports and put our visa papers under the windshield wipers of the vans while they were checking our entire luggage. Suddenly, a gust of wind blew one of the visas off the windshield, over the bridge, and into the river. Many negative thoughts immediately ran through my head: *Okay, I probably will have to take a train, along with the person who lost the visa, back to Vienna to get a new visa.* Most likely it would take more than a week, so it would really not even be an option.

"Clar Anderson hopped out of the van and looked over the railing into the two hundred-foot-wide river below. There was one rock about the size of a large suitcase in the middle of the river. Lying on top of the rock was the visa. The wind was howling, making ripples over the water, but the visa was staying on the rock. Clar somehow convinced the border guard to let him climb down an embankment into the river. It seemed like an eternity as I thought the visa would just blow it into the river. Miraculously, the totally dry paper visa was safely recovered. God has a unique way of demonstrating that He is in charge, and it was obviously clear to all of us as we watched in awe."

The wrestling team was beginning to spin off its work into multiple areas and other unique opportunities. By 1988, the ever-increasing expense and the expanding post-college wrestling club environment in the United States led the AIA national directors to decide to discontinue the full-time traveling wrestling teams. It had been an amazing twenty years of continuous competition and touring for the teams. It was now time for a strategic change of direction. But many wrestlers stayed on with AIA to advance the many other avenues to serve the sports ministries. A number of AIA wrestlers were asked to coach on various US international tournament teams. Colorado Springs became the AIA international headquarters, as the west team dissolved and left Southern California.

Summer camps for high school and middle school wrestlers became another strategic sports outreach to thousands of young kids in Colorado, California, Pennsylvania, Michigan, and other states, all guided by AIA wrestler Steve Burack. The combination of top coaches sharing spiritual principles and teaching wrestling skills, plus having all-out fun created lifelong memories for the camp attendees.

Here are some comments from the campers:

"The most important, touching, happiest, best, and wonderful week of my life."

"The discussions and talks have really made me think about committing my life to Christ."

"The talks moved me, and I wanted to be a follower of God."

"I was surprised to come here and see people so freely proclaim their Christianity."

"I love talking with other Christians because there aren't many at my school."

"I think the group leader helped me to know more about Jesus, God, and the Spirit. This is the best camp I have ever been to."

Even invited coaches were greatly impacted:

"I was first introduced to Steve Burack and AIA wrestling camps in 1997. I was touched by the strong commitment and Christian values held by Steve and John Peterson. Another great blessing is being able to minister to young impressionable kids who, in many cases, did not come from Christian homes. Many of these camp relationships have grown into life relationships as they went to college and adult life. My family and I are eternally grateful to the Lord for allowing me to be involved."

Over time, the full-time traveling teams were replaced by numerous effective sports outreaches all over the world and all led by former AIA wrestlers who chose not to "retire" after competing or go off to another career. Athletic talent can slowly fade away, but God's fully committed men and women will never fade.

Then suddenly the Iron Curtain fell!

"The fruit of the righteous is a tree of
life and he who is wise wins souls."
(Proverbs 22:30)

Chapter 12

To Russia with Love

One life wholly devoted to God is of more value than
one hundred lives simply awakened by His Spirit.
—Oswald Chambers

1991

In 1991 the AIA team continued to toil day and night in Europe. Carl and Noreen Dambman, along with Steve and Cindi Barrett, moved permanently to Moscow, as Russia opened up to newfound freedom. Other AIA wrestlers moved to the Czech Republic under the leadership of Reid and Carolyn Lamphere. The former relationships developed with the Czech wrestlers paid off handsomely. University students in Prague would come to a meeting room on campus just to hear Reid talk about the Bible and Christianity. All it took was passing out fliers on the campus grounds in the student commons area, since every student wanted to hear about the "taboo" subjects of Jesus and the Bible.

To go from decades of communist repression, secrecy, and fear to open-ended freedom and democracy was mind-boggling to the Russians and all the Soviet Bloc countries. Some people thrived while other found themselves "dependency slaves" to the old government ways.

Steve Barrett explains what the changes were like: "In the early 1990s, I was talking to a young man in Northern Russia and explaining to him our democratic system in America. I told him our forefathers used biblical principles to establish a civil government. Freedom meant that we could make decisions for ourselves. I explained to him that in Communism and Socialism the government offers an assortment of free programs for the citizens in areas like childcare, education, medical care, and various types of welfare programs. I also explained that every time the government gives us something for 'free,' it is one more choice they make for us and one less choice the individual makes for himself. In the extreme form of Soviet Communism, there is very little personal freedom, and most of life's decisions are made for individuals by the government.

"As we talked, he began to understand what I was trying to say, almost as though the light bulb of understanding went on. He said that while he was serving his two years of mandatory service in the Soviet army, 'They told me when to get up in the morning, when to go to bed, when to march, when to eat. Everything I did was regimented and dictated. When I got out of the army and came home, I stayed in my apartment for two weeks. I had completely lost my ability to make decisions for myself and was paralyzed.' He added, 'I think that is where our Russian society is now. We've been told what to do and think for so long. Now that we've got freedom, we don't have a clue what to do with it. We don't know how to make decisions anymore!'

"I've heard the following observation from more than one Russian: during the Soviet era, whatever wasn't allowed was forbidden. The opposite is true in America. Everything that isn't forbidden or against the law is allowed! This was another way the Russians were programmed to not venture outside of very strict parameters.

"Another saying during the Soviet system was, 'Any initiative will be punished.' The Soviet leadership was not looking for the masses to demonstrate initiative. They wanted people to follow orders, and they definitely didn't want them thinking for themselves, but to 'only believe'! My forefathers in the United States created a government that ensured freedom for each individual to make their own choices. God created us in His image, to be decision makers, giving each one of us personal responsibility."

AIA wrestlers understood freedom and lost no time in taking advantage of it. In 1991, AIA hooked up with a Christian soccer team, the Charlotte Eagles, from Charlotte, North Carolina. They toured Russia playing soccer teams and speaking to groups. In a three-week period, they distributed twenty thousand Bibles and thousands of Christian booklets all over Moscow and Kiev. Many Russians and Ukrainians had never even met an American, so to get a Bible of their own (which had been illegal for decades) was astounding to them. They took them and read them to learn about the God they had been taught did not exist. The days of sneaking Bibles across the borders and risk of being followed by the secret police were over!

Steve and fellow AIA wrestler Don Zellmer fully recognized how the political environment had changed. A couple years earlier they were visiting a city in Russia where they were mentoring some athletes using the Bible. They drove after dinner to meet their men in a more private location. After the Bible study ended they left in their car to go back to their hotel in the unfamiliar city. As they drove off, they noticed a car was following them, carefully staying about a city block behind. After a half-hour of driving around in circles not finding their hotel, they came up with a unique solution to solve their problem. They stopped their car, walked back to the car with the KGB agents, and asked them how to find their hotel. Amazingly, the stunned agents, trying to hide their cover, gave them directions and told them how to find their hotel!

Carl and Steve headed back to language school again, this time to learn Russian. Luckily for them McDonald's was already entrenched in Moscow, so to save time the staff team hired a local boy to buy hamburgers and french fries for their lunch. The taste of American junk food relieved pressure during the grueling Russian language classes with its very difficult Slavic alphabet. At least Steve and Carl knew some wrestling words, some words for food, and a few Biblical words. Within a few years of very difficult study, they were fluent in Russian.

Carl had an experience that vividly reveals how dramatic the culture had changed. In his own words, he illustrates the stark and radical contrast that came to Moscow: "In the early 1990s, I met a journalist who interviewed me about my Christian faith. I got a phone call from him and he said, 'Carl, the first professional hockey tournament is happening and we'd like you to come down. A Canadian hockey player by the name of Gordy Howe is here as a guest. We'd like you and Gordy to sit in what used to be Leonid Brezhnev's [former President of the Presidium of the Supreme Soviet] box seat.' Of course I was honored. Then he said, 'At the start of the tournament, we would like you to say a special blessing for all the hockey players and all the persons involved. Then at the end of the tournament, we'd also like you to say another special blessing. Oh, and this will also be on Soviet national television!'

"So one year I am being followed around by the secret police and can't talk to anybody … and a couple of years later I am on national television with a hundred million or more people watching … and I'm asked to give a special blessing! God is good! We also arranged to give away a Russian Bible to the first thousand people who sent in a request to the television station that was airing the event. Imagine the national television company distributing Bibles on our behalf. When I arrived in the parking lot, I asked if I could present a gift to the journalists, a Russian New Testament, and they agreed. The flood gates were open and everybody was interested."

Steve Barrett learned the hard way how difficult it was for a society held in a prisonlike culture under communism, to be infused with sudden freedom. Steve used sports to reach out to more than just elite athletes and coaches. He also had compassion for the down-and-out people—for the forgotten ones whose lives had been almost unbearable. Steve used wrestling to reach out to the downtrodden, but it was not always easy. Here is a story he shared of the hardship:

"We had permission from the main office and director of all the prisons in this region of Komi to visit the hospital prison Vislyana. It was a long drive, and when we got there the prison director would not talk with us. He sent his assistant to tell us we could not come in. This happens often, and you need to negotiate for a while and convince them that you aren't some kind of religious cult. As we were talking with the assistant director, he had a group of prison guards come in with billy clubs. When they came in, they were intentionally bumping into us, and the warden said there was no way he would let us in. As we were leaving, a Russian friend said, 'You are not rejecting us, you are rejecting God. We came on His behalf to speak to the (prisoners).'

"Six months later we heard of a prison where no Christians had ever visited. It was a long way from any town and very difficult to reach. We headed for this prison early in the morning and had driven several hours to a point where there was a turnoff leading there. Nobody had driven on this road since the last snowstorm, and there was a couple of feet of snow on the ground. There was no way our vehicle could make it. As we started to head back, I asked, 'Aren't we close to Vislyana, the hospital prison?' Another Russian friend said, 'Yes, but there's no way we are going there. You remember how they treated us last time?' I said, 'We don't have a lot else to do, so let's give it a try.'

"When we got to the prison and they saw who we were, the new director came out to meet us and eagerly said, 'Come into my office and tell me what you need!' We said we wanted to get all the prisoners together in one place, and we wanted a general announcement inviting all the prisoners to the meeting. He gave the command to his guards to set our requests in motion. We had a great meeting with the guys. They were very attentive, and a lot of them came forward and crowded around us to pray to receive Christ. I've been to a lot of different prisons with Dr. Beau Jennings doing clinics for inmates. You have to be very sick to be taken out of a prison and put into a prison hospital. A lot of the guys had tuberculosis, and because of lack of medicine they were not going to get well.

"We found out as we were leaving what had happened during those six months between visits. Two days after our first visit the prison director, who would not see us, the assistant director, who was rude to us, and a couple of the guards who had come in during their show of force were in an automobile accident. All of them died except for the assistant director, who was paralyzed from the neck down. Everyone in the prison had attributed it to the words of my Russian friend who said, 'You are not rejecting us, you are rejecting God!' The atmosphere had completely changed, and the new director did not want to be responsible for keeping anyone from hearing what we came to say."

Russia and the old Soviet Bloc countries today are much more adjusted to a sense of freedom but are no longer fascinated by the newness of meeting Americans with Bibles. However, the AIA sports outreach continues using more traditional sports ministry strategies. Many athletes in Russia and the old Soviet countries now manage their own sports ministries, thanks to the relentless efforts of the wrestlers who were committed to training athletes in the ways of God and the strategies of sports ministry. Never will athletes and coaches lose their ability to use their popularity and respect to share their faith with other people. AIA wrestlers and the men and women they have mentored will always be there as the catalyst to train, teach, and encourage others. The legacy lives on!

> "A friend loves at all times, and a
> brother is born for adversity."
> (Proverbs 17:17)

Chapter 13

The End of the Beginning

When we realize Jesus Christ has served us to the end of His
measure for our selfishness and sin, nothing that we meet from
others can exhaust our determination to serve men for His sake.
—Oswald Chambers

2014
Going Forward

By the summer of 1988, the full-time Athletes in Action wrestling teams had finished their amazing run. For twenty consecutive years they had competed successfully against the best wrestlers in the United States and with the elite wrestlers around the world. During those two decades, more than 110 men had wrestled for AIA in competition. They had competed in more than 253 dual meets against many of the best US college teams with a win-loss record of an amazing 215–36–2, winning 85 percent of the time. Their athletes won three Olympic medals and had a dozen wrestlers compete internationally for the United States on 15 different teams. They were US National Freestyle team champions three different times. They were 1–0 in wrestling club dual meets, defeating their rival New York Athletic Club. They were 0–1 against the world silver medalist Polish Greco-Roman wrestling team. They had competed in dozens of countries around the world. They were respected by every wrestling coach and wrestling federation in the world for their athletic success and their integrity both on and off the mat.

Their athletic prowess was truly outstanding, and the success provided them credibility and a public platform. However, the most important thing in the end was their spiritual impact, not their physical prowess. Eternal impact trumps physical impact. Serving God to impact people's eternal destiny trumps impressing people with medals and victories. They were true ambassadors for the sport they loved and for the Lord they served.

With this priority the AIA wrestlers did not end their sports careers just because the teams ceased traveling. Far from it! They simply adjusted their strategies and pressed on, just as the apostle Paul suggested in describing his spiritual life: "But one thing I do; forgetting what lies behind and reaching forward to what lies ahead, I press on toward the goal for the prize of the upward call of God in Christ Jesus" (Philippians 3:13–14).

AIA wrestlers continue to this day to provide leadership in many of AIA's sports ministries, particularly on the international front. The years of thinking globally had given these mature men a special niche in reaching others with the Good News of Christ. AIA wrestler Reid Lamphere has traveled to 124 countries—so far! It all started when AIA came to wrestle his team at the University of Minnesota. He was hooked as soon as he heard the wrestlers' message of Jesus Christ. God led him to join AIA after graduation from college. A few years later he wrestled in Iran on the 1977 AIA tour in the Aryamehr Cup. Even though he had wrestled internationally twice in the World Championships in 1974 and 1977, Reid had an experience in Iran that created the spark when he felt God pulling him toward an international destiny.

He remembers vividly when it happened: "I was able to compete in one of the most prestigious wrestling tournaments in the world—the Aryamehr Cup—which was actually hosted by the Shah of Iran. We arrived a few days early in Tehran and spent most of the time training and preparing for the competition. One day we took a couple of hours to go to the central market to see the teeming masses of locals shopping for every possible thing on earth. We hadn't been in the market more than ten minutes when we walked by two old men sitting on the ground, leaning against the wall at the market. At that time, Iranians seemed to love Americans and we thought nothing of wearing our US warm-up jackets. Seeing us with our US clothing, one of the men called out, 'USA!' I stopped and looked at him. Then he said, "Category" (referring to the weight class I wrestled). I replied, "Sixty-two kilo," and he just stared at me. Then I realized he didn't speak English. The word "category" is kind of an international word in the world of wrestling. So I held up six fingers and then two fingers, signifying that I wrestle at 62 kilograms (136.5 pounds). He paused for a moment and then said, 'Lamphere!' I couldn't believe my ears. Some random guy sitting on the street in Tehran knew my name. He had obviously read the newspaper containing the lineup for the various countries and had memorized all the names of the Americans. I felt God's call to use my talent to reach into parts of the world that were closed to the message of Christ. The planting of those tiny seeds was enough to make God's call very clear within the next few months."

Reid led the US east team to Europe within a year of the Iran trip. He and his wife, Carolyn, spent the next fifteen years in Europe reaching out to people through wrestling while raising two children in Austria, Germany, and Czechoslovakia.

In the midnineties, Reid and Carolyn felt it was the right time to return to the United States. They landed in Atlanta to head up a coalition of churches and a Christian organization to minister in the 1996 Olympic games. Reid was the perfect man to lead the project, which included other AIA staff members from around the world. The AIA wrestling team alumni also decided to hold a reunion in Atlanta to gather about fifty of the teammates and families for some fellowship. Reid had been involved in the original Olympic project in 1972 in Munich, but he was not quite sure how to lead a project successfully twenty-four years later! Some would call it "flying by the seat of your pants," while others would call it trusting God to lead you when there are no clear solutions in sight.

Here is how Reid tells the story as he implemented both trusting God and flying by the seat of his pants: "One of my roles during the Atlanta Olympics was to organize the ministry outreach for our own Athletes in Action Olympic project, which was comprised of 110 people. One of the key distinctions of AIA is to focus on the elite athlete at the Games. Therefore, I wanted our 110 staff and volunteers (from 22 countries) to be able to actually minister to all Olympians. The problem was that I didn't have a clue as to how our staff would be able to directly contact members of the Olympic Family. About 15,000 Olympians were housed in a secured Olympic Village and then they were transported in a secured bus to the competition venues and back to the Village again. My only hope was that, at some point, some of them would venture out of the Village and one of our people would meet them on the streets. Our AIA leadership kept asking me if we had a plan to reach the athletes and I assured them we did. I didn't go into detail … because there was no detail. The only plan was to trust God to do something. But I was living under considerable 'pressure to perform' and it didn't feel good.

"At the same time The Jesus Film Project asked me if I thought we would be able to give Jesus videos to the Olympic athletes. I told them we could definitely do it, so they gave us a thousand videos for free. The bargain price at that time was $10 per video. So here I sat with $10,000 worth of videos and the entire *Jesus Film* organization watching to see if we were going to deliver. More pressure.

"One day the phone rang. It was a former CRU staff member who had a program on a Christian radio station in Texas. He said he would try to raise an additional $10,000 so that we could buy a thousand more videos and wanted to know if I thought we could get them to the athletes. I exclaimed to myself, 'Definitely!' The truth was I had not one bit of faith that we could even meet two thousand Olympians and distribute all of those videos. I knew that saying yes would create yet more pressure and stress, but how could you turn down $10,000 worth of free quality gifts for the Olympians that could impact their lives?

"When I woke up on the first day of our Olympic project, I honestly felt the same as I would on the morning of a major wrestling match. My adrenalin was flowing, my heart was beating fast, and my head was as clear as a bell. On the day before our 110 staff were to descend on Atlanta in the hopes of meeting athletes, I decided to send one person into the city to spend a half-day and see what would happen—to see how possible it was to meet athletes.

"Later that evening this guy approached me with a big smile on his face. He told me how he had been able to meet an Olympian from the Seychelles Islands and the guy gladly received one of the *Jesus Films* from him. A surge of relief and excitement shot through me. I was so happy that the strategy was going to work. We had actually had a conversation with an Olympic athlete and had put one of the Jesus videos in his hands. But the elation was short-lived when I realized we still had 1,999 videos left in dozens of boxes in our temporary headquarters location.

"The next morning came and the AIA troops were ready to go to battle. We had given everyone a backpack to use to transport the videos. Remember, this was in the day before DVD and the old VHS cassettes were about twenty times the size and heavier than the modern DVD. That meant that each person could only take a few videos with them each day. We had fifty different languages of the *Jesus Film* and this presented a dilemma as to which languages to carry that day. Each person took several English and a few each of the other major languages (Spanish, French, Russian, German, etc.). This left little room for any of the more exotic languages. But we prayed together daily that God would direct us. And then we went out to see what God would do.

"On the first day, one of our guys threw into his backpack a Polish and a Bulgarian video. The first two guys he ran into were from Poland and Bulgaria. Another guy, Tom, left with several in

Spanish, one in Hungarian, and one in Swahili (even though he had no idea where Swahili was spoken). He gave away his Hungarian video within the first hour. Then he met a group of Spanish athletes and gave each one a copy. While he was doing this, he noticed an athlete standing nearby watching what was going on. After the Spanish athletes left, Tom asked the guy standing there if he would like one also. The athlete replied, 'I think you will not have one in my language.' Tom asked him what language he speaks and he replied, 'Swahili' (he was from Kenya). Tom reached into his backpack and pulled out his one Swahili video and handed it over. His eyes got wide and he kept saying, 'This really talks in my language?' We discovered in the festive Olympic environment that everyone was friendly as they wore their countries' colors or insignia and were eager to meet others to exchange greetings and even gifts.

"Another AIA staffer was on his way back to our headquarters after a long day in the city. He had met many athletes on the streets, had great conversations about spiritual things and had given all of his videos away except for three—two in Arabic and one in Hindi. While walking to the subway he passed by a bus stop where athletes waited for a ride back to the Olympic Village. He noticed two guys standing there wearing uniforms from the country of Qatar. He had no idea what language they spoke, so he asked them. They replied, 'We speak Arabic.' He was further amazed at the way God worked as he gave away his last two videos. But just then one other athlete walked up and asked, 'Do you have a video for me?' Our staffer said, 'I'm sorry, but I don't have any more videos in Arabic.' The athlete said, 'I don't speak Arabic. I speak Hindi.' He pulled out his final Jesus video and gave it to the athlete from India. The day's mission was accomplished!

"I can't begin to tell you how many times this has happened. With six days left of the Olympics we gave away the last of our two thousand videos. Our project members started calling friends and financial supporters to ask if they would contribute $100 to buy ten more videos. In the end, we didn't run out of money, but rather we ran out of foreign-language Jesus videos. We had purchased every foreign language *Jesus Film* in North America and have given out more than thirty-five hundred videos in fifty different languages to athletes from more than one hundred countries."

Reid and Carolyn now have outreach projects at almost all of the major international sports competitions—the Pan Am, the Asian, the All-Africa, the World University Games, etc. God uses these major athletic competitions, which provide an athletic friendly environment to do miraculous things to open doors in the athletic world through meeting key people from all over the world.

Reid reports, "A few years ago I was at the Central American and Caribbean Games—an event with about four thousand athletes competing in twenty-three sports from thirty-plus countries. One day I was walking across the Athletes' Village with our AIA staff guy from Honduras, Marco Antonio. We happened to run into the president of the Olympic Committee for Honduras. Marco Antonio spoke to him and the president asked us to join him for breakfast in the cafeteria.

"When we told him we were with an organization called Athletes in Action, he asked, 'What could Athletes in Action do to help sport in Honduras?'

"I replied, 'First of all, we could send AIA teams to Honduras to compete. Or we could host teams from Honduras in the United States. But the thing that we are especially equipped to do is to help athletes develop the spiritual part of their lives—to become a whole person physically, mentally, and spiritually.'

"The president looked at us and said, 'I'd like Marco Antonio to do that for the athletes of Honduras. We are about to open a new Olympic training center, and I'd like Marco Antonio to work with the athletes at this new center.'

"By attending that one sport event, Marco Antonio was thrust into a position of influence and spiritual ministry that would have probably taken him a decade to achieve—if ever. And this is something that we see at *every* event we go to. The door does not always open as wide as it did for Marco Antonio, but one or more of our staff or a volunteer always gets elevated to a position of greater opportunity. There's something about just being at these events that helps create opportunities. Obviously, each of these door-opening experiences is preceded by a divine appointment—by the moving of the Holy Spirit—to bring our staff to just the right place at just the right time. And, again, I'm totally convinced that this is happening in response to a great backing of prayer by hundreds of faithful prayer supporters back home."

In London at the 2012 Olympic Games, 180 Christian sports men and women from three dozen countries went out into the city streets daily for ten straight days talking to athletes, coaches, and sports fans about Jesus. They gave out 5,000 DVDs. Each DVD was presented as a gift, which could be viewed in any of 36 different languages, showing Olympic athletes in different sports from different countries sharing their personal stories of how Jesus Christ had changed their lives. Almost a dozen of the former AIA wrestlers and wives were there walking the streets of London.

What motivated Reid to circle the globe and set up various large outreach projects in foreign lands to reach out to people who were strangers to him? Simple answer: The love of Christ! It never gets old! God's love is infinite, powerful, and fully motivating! Seeing God change a life is exhilarating! The fact that God can use any ordinary person to be the channel of His love is astounding. And every human being, regardless of country, has the same basic needs—peace, forgiveness, meaning, and purpose. Since anyone is a candidate to hear the story, the AIA men and women never have to force the issue because it is free.

Perhaps it is very simple to explain. It could be the sheer joy … that God can use a wrestler to effectively change a life for the good. In the early AIA wrestling team days, Reid and Brian Dameier spoke in a high school assembly, and they received a letter from an audience participant: "First, I'd like to share my experience with God with you. After Reid had said his prayer, I asked God to come into my life.

And then I felt all cold and a tingle went down my back. I wanted to shout with joy. Then my life changed. Before it didn't seem to have any meaning, but after my acceptance I felt much better. The days became brighter. But it wasn't until recently that I realized I had accepted God. Now I find myself having long talks with God. I am continually praying and praising God. I want to thank you with all my heart. You have opened my eyes to a world that I never really realized before."

In Beijing at the 2008 Olympic Games, several AIA wrestlers and a few other former athletes decided to go to the International Church to worship on Sunday morning. This church is off limits to the local Chinese people, by government mandate. Only internationals can attend by showing their passport at the door. The service was mostly in English, and there were several hundred people there. One special guest presented a short play on the amazing life of Eric Liddell, whose life was featured in the Oscar-winning movie *Chariots of Fire*. Eric Liddell was an Olympic champion in the 1922 games. He was the son of Scottish missionaries based in China and became famous because he refused to run and compete in his event, the 100 meters, on a Sunday—the Lord's Day. But after some negotiations with his coach, he was allowed to run in the 400 meters race on another day, and Eric Liddell won a gold medal. An interesting fact we learned that day in China was that Eric Liddell was born in China and thus became the first Chinese-born athlete to win an Olympic gold medal.

Soon after the Olympics, Eric went back to China to work as a missionary. While in China, he developed a sports ministry and loved working with children, teaching them track and field while sharing the love of Christ with them. He even refereed soccer and rugby games for these kids so he could share his faith with them. Eric Liddell may have won the gold for Great Britain, but he led untold numbers of people to Christ through his Christian work. He eventually died in China as a prisoner of war in a Japanese camp during World War II.

Flash forward ninety years to the London Games. On Friday, August 9, 2012, the first ever More than Gold Legacy Breakfast was held in the beautiful Methodist Central Hall across from Westminster Abbey. More than Gold sponsored the event and is an international sport ministry that AIA wrestlers helped facilitate years earlier, which pulls together all the various athletic ministries around the world. Many sports celebrities attended the breakfast along with a number of Olympic coaches and athletes. The event was free to Olympians, and tickets to the event were given out by AIA Olympic project volunteers. Several hundred people filled the beautiful large room as breakfast was served and several keynote speakers honored the life of Eric Liddell.

Two special guests were Eric Liddell's daughters, Trish and Heather, now in their seventies. The sisters gave the Eric Liddell Award to two Olympians who exhibited top performances in specific sports, integrity in their lifestyle, and the same Christian character as their father.

Eric Liddell was likely one of the first athletes who strategically used his sports fame to share the gospel of Jesus Christ. What a legacy! How excited he would have been to see the AIA Olympic project team in London—all 180 of them from 38 countries—proclaiming Christ every day to athletes, coaches and fans. As he said to his sister in the movie when he tried out for the British Olympic team, "God made me fast. He made me that way for a reason. I can honor God with my running."

This story is not over; not even close. In fact, the victories will continue to be won, one person at a time, as God continues to use wrestlers "to win for thee the victory and from thee the victor's crown."

> "For the Lord of hosts has planned, and who can frustrate
> it? As for His stretched out hand, who can turn it back?"
> (Isaiah 14:27)

Epilogue

The history of the Athletes in Action wrestling team is a compelling one. Often, God does something unique in history which is never to be repeated again. He sometimes uses the least likely person or group of people to impact the world with the message of His love. In approximately 1,000 BC, when God chose an obscure shepherd boy named David to become king of Israel, it is recorded that while David was fleeing for his life from King Saul, a group of men gathered under his leadership. Note the description of the men in I Samuel 22:2: "And everyone who was in distress, and everyone who was in debt, and everyone who was discontented gathered." They were quite a motley crew. But years later, in II Samuel 23 near the end of David's life, some of these very same men were described as David's "mighty men," who were famous for all the incredible things they did with David for God's glory.

God can create anything out of nothing when He chooses to move into the lives of men and women. Once He starts to move, no one could ever guess the results. And no one can stop Him either!

Such is the story of the mighty men of the Athletes in Action wrestling team. It started as an idea, a vision, and a dream of one man, Dave Hannah. God then gathered a small group of athletes and their wives to create a traveling team of competing wrestlers. They were average, normal men who had a talent to wrestle on the mat. Although wrestling was the first Olympic sport along with track in 776 BC, it is considered a minor sport in many countries, including the United States. No one was paying particular attention when the first recruits gathered in June 1968 to determine if a team of Christian athletes could be formed to share the message of Christ. No one could have fathomed the results.

Over the course of 20 years, 110 college wrestlers joined the AIA team to tour all over the world and share their faith. They were champions on and off the mat as they wrestled "for the glory of God." They personally talked to an estimated 1.5 million people about how to know Jesus Christ in a personal way. Everywhere they competed, the media reported to millions of sports fans about this unique team. Tens of thousands of people responded to their message by committing their lives to Christ.

Today, many of the former wrestlers are involved in numerous sports ministry reaching out to people all over the world. Over the years their methods have changed, but their message has stayed the same—that God loves you, and you need to allow Christ into your personal life. Thousands more each year continue to hear them speak and are influenced by their lives to this day. Nothing will ever stop their message. Their history is not finished. Ten wrestlers continue to work for AIA or CRU today.

As the apostle Paul said in I Corinthians 1:26–27, "Brothers, think of what you were when you were called. Not many of you were wise by human standard; not many were influential; not many were of noble birth. But God chose the foolish things of the world to confound the wise."

In His Grip,
Greg Hicks

Greg Hicks and Gene and Frances Davis cheer
the US team at the 2008 Olympics in China.

Several of the original AIA wrestlers join
young AIA wrestlers from Canada, Poland, and
Mongolia at the London Olympics, 2012.

Afterword

AIA Wrestling Match Halftime and High
School Assembly Presentation, 1970s
Greg Hicks

Recently, *Life* magazine took a national survey. In this survey, the question was asked, "What do you want most in life?" Eighty-eight out of one hundred people said, "I want to have peace within, and I want to be honest with other people."

Why do you suppose they have this need? Why do we not have peace of mind, and why do we condemn hypocrisy and yet play the game ourselves?

We, on this wrestling team, believe the answer lies in the fact that most people do not understand how to have a personal relationship with Jesus Christ. Jesus himself said, "I came that they might have life and have it more abundantly." (John 10:10)

There is no real peace today. There is violence, hatred, and never-ending war. But the real war lies within the hearts of men. There is prejudice, frustration, restlessness, loneliness, and worst of all, guilt. All of us are guilty, and all of us desperately need forgiveness. Today, fifty-two percent of our hospital beds are filled with "mental patients," and psychologists tell us that most of the patients are there because of guilt! The Bible says we want to do what is right, but we have no power to do so. This causes guilt and frustration. The Bible also says, "For all have sinned and come short of the glory of God," and "the wages of sin is death." (Romans 3:23 & 6:23)

This is why Jesus Christ becomes the most important person in history and why no one can afford to ignore Him. He said two thousand years ago, "Peace I leave with you, my peace I give unto you, not as the world gives, do I give unto you; let not your heart be troubled, neither let it be afraid!" (John 14:27)

But most people today think Christianity is either an emotional fanatical experience or a religion that takes all the fun out of life. They have reduced it to a code of ethics or a rule of life. Has it ever occurred to you that Christianity is not a religion but a relationship—a relationship with the resurrected Jesus Christ?

Jesus said, "God is Spirit and those who worship Him must worship in spirit and truth." (John 4:24) Just as we were born physically to begin our natural life, we begin our spiritual life with a spiritual birth. Experiencing a spiritual birth begins a relationship with Christ. But God is holy and just and demands that we fulfill His laws. The only problem is that we cannot!

An illustration is helpful. Suppose you are arrested for speeding and taken to court. Your father happens to be the judge. The father knows justice must be done and the penalty for breaking the law must be paid. But your father loves you. The penalty is thirty dollars or ten days in jail, and you have no money. The father then takes off his robe, puts down his gavel, comes to the front of the bench, pulls out his wallet, and pays the fine. Thus justice is satisfied, the penalty is paid, and you go free. That is exactly what God has done for us. He has paid the debt, setting us free. "But God demonstrates His love for us in that while we were yet sinners, Christ died for us." (Romans 5:8)

But how do we experience this new birth and begin a personal relationship with Christ? Christ makes it very clear when he said, "Behold, I stand at the door and knock (the door of our mind, emotions, and will); if any man opens the door, I will come into him." (Revelation 3:20) So God does not want us to perform for Him but wants us to ask Christ to come into our lives and take residence. But God does not want to force us to be spiritual robots or puppets, so he gives us the free choice of whether to accept or reject Christ as our personal savior.

Some of you may be thinking, look, Greg, this sounds too simple.

The reason it is so simple for us is because it costs God so much. It is our hope that each of you will seriously consider this life-changing commitment to Jesus Christ.

It is our custom to not only talk about Christ but to give each of you the same opportunity that someone once gave each of us—an opportunity to receive Jesus Christ. If you would like to begin a personal relationship with Jesus Christ, you can open the door of your life right now. We do this by talking to God through prayer. Let's pray. "Lord Jesus, come into my life, forgive my sins, and take control of my life. Make me the kind of person I really desire to be. Thank you for coming in as You promised. Amen."

If you just asked Christ to come into your life, He is there. The Christian life is not a matter of feelings but a matter of fact. He will begin to revolutionize your life from the inside out, as you trust Him.

And now I would like for you to take out your small comment card, and I want to tell you how you can really help us. Please comment honestly about what you heard tonight. Some of you may like it; some may not, but be honest with us and tell us what you think. Some of you said that prayer and if you did, would you tell us or put a check mark by your name? And if you want some information, we would love to send you some, so give us your name and address, and we will send you some helpful material. Someone will take up the cards in just a moment. Thank you so much for listening to us!

Appendix A

Information on Athletes in Action Wrestling

The AIA wrestling team story is challenging and compelling. Many people instinctively want to learn more and support a movement that is having such a positive impact on people throughout the world through sports, athletes, and coaches.

The Athletes in Action headquarters is located near Cincinnati, Ohio, and has an international and wrestling office in Colorado Springs, Colorado. The AIA website is www.athletesinaction.org.

If you specifically want to show your support financially to the wrestling ministry outreaches and projects, you can send a tax deductible contribution to:

Athletes in Action
"AIA Wrestling Scholarships" (Account # 2825649)
651 Taylor Drive
Xenia, Ohio 45385

If you have a comment about the book, have met an AIA wrestler personally, or have heard them speak publicly, you may want to go to their Facebook page AIA Wrestling Book (https://www.facebook.com/pages/AIA-Wrestling-Book/212213042305408) and make a comment. The AIA wrestlers will be interested in your comments and will perhaps respond to you. The team members would be especially interested in your comments if you ever came in contact with them, and specifically how your life may have been affected by their presentation to you in years past.

Be sure to watch a terrific wrestling video of some of today's wrestlers talking about their commitment to wrestling and to their Lord: http://beyondtheultimate.org/DVD/unfading-glory.aspx.

Appendix B

Athletes in Action Wrestlers

Gary Almquist
Larry Amundson
Bob Anderson
James Axtell
Stephen Barrett
Casey Bartels
Loren Baum
Tim Berry
Bruce Bulman
Steve Burak
Ray Caldwell
Anthony Califano
Nick Carollo
Jesse Castro
Hector Cedillo
Tim Celek
Rick Clark
Allyn Cooke
Murray Crews
Dan Cuestas
Carl Dambman
Brian Dameier
Gene Davis

Mark Dymond
Mike Erb
Mike Evans
Greg Fetzer
Keith Fisher
Steve Gaydosh
Joe George
Bill Gifford
Rick Greene
John Hansen
Frank Harl
Tom Harrington
John Hart
JD Hawkins
Rich Hay
Dan Hicks
Greg Hicks
Sam Hieronymus
Art Holden
Art Hollands
Colin Hudson
Jon Jackson
Tom Keeley

Scottie Kendle
John Klein
Doug Klenovich
Bob Kuhn
★Kent Kershner
Reid Lamphere
Tom Lamphere
John Lightner
John Lowe
Jon Lundberg
William Martin
Steve Maurey
Carnie McArthur
Michael McArthur
★Mike McCready
Cam McElhany
Loren Miller
Mike Moore
Dan Morrison
Dan Moskowitz
Kyung MuChang
Karl Mulle
Dave Mulnix

Rafe Mumford

Pat Murphy

Mitsu Nakai

Pete Noble

Greg Okoorian

Jay Olinger

Joe Padraza

Phil Paladay

John Peterson

Rich Pollock

Jim Porter

Dave Pratt

Dave Redd

Ed Rew

Doug Rickard

Tom Riley

Steve Ross

Gary Rushing

Rick Seilhamer

Henry Shaffer

Dan Sherman

Don Shuler

Joe Sloan

Doug Smith

Wayne Smith

Kevin Sorensen

Steve Suder

Tom Talbert

Gary Taylor

Aaron Thomas

Neil Turner

Bob Walker

Gary Wallman

Dan Warren

*John Weber

Mike West

Drew Whitfield

Mike Whitfield

Jarrett Williman

Jody Zeller

Don Zellmer

*Deceased

Appendix C
Journal Entries

Amazingly, I kept my journals from this time period, and below is a sample month to show the pace at which we lived and worked. During the month of January 1972, the team covered thirty-eight hundred miles and had eight matches and forty-two speaking engagements to an estimated fourteen thousand people. During the month, I only had two free days!—Greg Hicks

January 1972

Saturday, January 1
- Leave the Atlanta College Student Conference and travel from Atlanta to Greensboro, NC

Sunday, January 2
- Attend church

Monday, January 3
- Prayer letters
- Practice
- Speak at Bible Study

Tuesday, January 4
- Visit supporters
- Prayer letters
- Practice

Wednesday, January 5
- Visit supporters
- Practice

Thursday, January 6
- Personal study
- Practice
- Get car fixed

Friday, January 7
- Travel from Greensboro, NC to University of VA Charlottesville
- Practice

Saturday, January 8
- Staff meeting
- Weigh-in
- Match against University of VA

Sunday, January 9
- Speak to adult Sunday School class
- Practice

Monday, January 10
- Speak at three gym classes (500 people)
- Travel to Clarion, PA

Tuesday, January 11
- Personal study
- Practice
- Free time

Wednesday, January 12
- Speak to three high school assemblies (1600 people; 502 decisions)

Thursday, January 13
- Travel to West Point, NY
- Practice

Friday, January 14
- Staff Bible study
- Weigh-in
- Match against Army (500 people)

Saturday, January 15
- Practice
- Travel to Springfield, MA

Sunday, January 16
- Church with Steve
- Practice
- Church talk

Monday, January 17
- Practice

- Match against Springfield; (1,000 people; 17 decisions)

Tuesday, January 18
- Travel to Long Island
- Weigh-in
- Match against NYAC (2,000 people)

Wednesday, January 19
- Travel to Clarion
- Personal study
- Team reports
- Staff team meeting

Thursday, January 20
- Staff Bible study
- Practice
- Match against Slip Rock (900 people)

Friday, January 21
- Office work
- Practice
- Match against W. Chest (2,000 people)

Saturday, January 22
- Free day

Sunday, January 23
- Speak at Dubois, PA church, radio
- Practice
- Team Bible study

Monday, January 24
- Travel to State College
- Practice—Penn State
- Fraternity meeting (20 people)

- Athletic AG (12 people)

Tuesday, January 25
- Breakfast
- Campus newspaper
- Practice
- College Life (300 people)

Wednesday, January 26
- Practice
- Travel to Loch Haven, PA
- Match against Loch Haven (1,000 people)
- Travel to River Ridge

Thursday, January 27
- Two high school assemblies (1,200 people; 275 decisions)
- Practice

Friday, January 28
- Reports
- Practice
- Team reception

Saturday, January 29
- Free day

Sunday, January 30
- Church—Clarion (250 people)

Monday, January 31
- Team Bible study
- Weigh-in
- Match against Clarion (2,500 people)